Cleopatra's RICHES

Cleopatra's RICHES

How to Earn, Grow, and Enjoy Your Money to Enrich Your Life

MARTHA ADAMS

Waterside Productions

Cardiff-by-the-Sea, California

Printed in the United States of America

Third Printing, 2022

ISBN-13: 978-1-949001-97-6 hardcover edition
ISBN-13: 978-1-949003-30-7 paperback edition
ISBN-13: 978-1-949003-31-4 ebook edition
ISBN-13: 978-1-949003-60-4 audiobook edition

Waterside Productions
2055 Oxford Avenue
Cardiff-by-the-Sea, CA 92007
www.waterside.com

To my parents, who showed me love before they even knew me.
Thank you for everything you did for me and for everything you taught me.
I love you, Baba and Mama.

Contents

Foreword

BY BOB PROCTOR

Most of us grow up with the idea that finances and self-development are two completely different things. As a result, it seems perfectly natural to feel connected to our inner selves when we talk about developing spiritually or intellectually, but not when we talk about our money. Money is almost viewed as being taboo in terms of people talking about it; it makes people uncomfortable. It's almost as if we're dealing with something that's outside of us. And that makes it harder for us to make significant improvements in that area of our life because we feel disconnected from it.

The ideas you'll find in this book will change all that. No matter who you are, instead of feeling lost, stuck, or disconnected, you will be able to step forward in a way that creates real and lasting change in your money story.

I get really jazzed when I meet people who really understand how money works. And Martha Adams is one of those people. I've known Martha for several years, and I feel lucky to have had the opportunity to become familiar with her great work.

I was pleased when Martha told me she was writing this book because she and her clients continually practice what you are about to read. And, consequently, they know how to earn, grow, and enjoy a tremendous amount of money.

Cleopatra's Riches clearly and effectively demonstrates something that I've been teaching for decades: You can't change your results by focusing on your current circumstances. If you focus on your current results, you'll continue to get more of the same. Martha understands that to improve your money story, you must first change your thoughts and feelings about money.

Martha also understands one more critical factor in creating and managing wealth. She realizes that joyfully earning more money is far less about strategy, and much more about your mindset. That's why she created practices such as "emotionalizing to the positive" and the "4R process."

Nearly 60 years ago, I was fortunate enough to have Napoleon Hill's book, *Think and Grow Rich*, put in my hands. That book changed my life forever. I'd like to share something Hill said about the power of our emotions.

Hill said, *"It is your responsibility to make sure that positive emotions constitute the dominating influence of your mind."*

I still read *Think and Grow Rich* every day because the ideas are sound. Well, the ideas in this book about wealth are sound too.

Martha has done a wonderful job of conveying her own success-generating ideas for you to follow. By weaving the essence of her 4R process into each page of this book, she has charted a clear path for you to earn more money, grow your money, and enjoy your money in the ways you want.

Don't just read this book; act on it. The only way for change to occur is though new and different action. Martha has applied these ideas to every stage of her own life, and she puts them into practice with her clients as a Certified Financial Planning Professional. If you do exactly what Martha suggests in each chapter, you'll be able to create the meaningful and lasting wealth-building changes you desire in your life.

Bob Proctor,
Best-selling author of *You Were Born Rich*

Introduction

The search for self-identity and a sense of belonging is a journey many of us take as we seek out purpose, meaning, and knowledge of ourselves—and our self-identity and money stories are more interconnected than we would think. At first glance, it would appear that I'm talking about two completely different things: finances and self-development. But the truth is, they're one and the same. The idea of self-identity is one that we can understand, connect, and relate to because it's within us. But when we haven't connected with ourselves, we can have what feels like a blank space. With an innate need to fill that space, it's natural for us to look toward external influences, opinions, and suggestions to fill in the gaps.

In my own search for identity, I found myself continually gravitating to the richness and beauty of my cultural ancestry. It was in that connection where I felt a sense of belonging. As a child, I would listen with pride and joy every time my mom told me that I was a direct descendant of Cleopatra. It was an anchor for me whenever the feelings of being different or "less than" in the community where I grew up would take hold. My connection to my ancestry was the way I started to practice what I call "emotionalizing to the positive." Essentially, I made the decision to view my experiences as positive rather than negative. Choosing positive emotions is a learned skill that needs to be nurtured.

This is what I'm sharing with you here today, using my own experiences to illustrate the concepts I'm presenting. It's because of the skill of emotionalizing to the positive, which I have applied to every stage of my own life, that I've been able to develop these concepts through my passion as an educator and put them into practice with my clients as a Certified Financial Planning Professional. I was able to focus my wealth management practice on teaching my clients how to *earn, grow,* and *enjoy* their money in the way they wanted. All of this is built on a strong foundation of positive emotions and a positive sense of self—something I sought for myself and instilled in those I've worked with.

When we talk about our money or our finances, we seem to lose ourselves in the numbers. And we become disconnected when we don't understand them. It's that void of knowledge and clear understanding that we're looking to fill with external messages. When we haven't found ourselves, or we don't have a positive relationship to ourselves, we look to everything and everyone else for answers. We seek out direction, not guidance. The difference between those two terms is significant. When we seek direction, we're looking outside ourselves for a defined path. We want someone or something else to point us in the right direction. On the other hand, guidance starts within us, and those around us will enhance that knowledge. In other words, when we know who we are and what we want, asking for guidance will serve to uplift us and move us forward on our journeys.

When it comes to money, searching for your identity and solutions outside of yourself is what you've been taught to do. But this will only cause you to be stuck in a negative loop, no matter what you do to try to get out of it and move forward. This is profoundly true when you think about your current financial situation. You're feeling stuck, but you can't figure out how to get out of this negative cycle. The problem is that you don't see yourself at the center of the loop. But now, let's shift the financial conversation around and talk about money starting from *within you.* Your money story is inside of you, and so is your *relationship* with money. So it would only make sense that the journey toward positive change starts with you! Your feelings and beliefs about money are within you—they are unique only to you, but you must understand where they came from in order to change the result. You already have the tools to make these positive changes in your life, and through self-development work, I'm going to show you how to apply them.

It doesn't matter who you are or what career or life path you're on, money is a central part of your life. It's also an aspect of your life that the majority of people have in common—and not just in the present, but throughout the generations, tracing all the way back to your origins. Even with money being central to your life, it's the topic in which you probably see yourself the least—instead, focusing on everything and everyone else. It all seems so unapproachable, distant, confusing, and incomplete. But I'm here to tell you that those feelings and beliefs don't have to remain. It's in that spirit that I'm honored to sit with you and share my passion to bring that positive shift to all aspects of money in your life. This is a shift that I firmly believe is possible and achievable—by *you*.

This belief that I have in your success, using the processes and tools I will share with you here, didn't just appear out of thin air. They arose through the application of a process I've developed and have continued to implement over the years. I created this process by combining my study of business, finance, and education in a meaningful way. It was the combination of my degrees and practical experience in these areas that allowed me to build my comprehensive wealth management practice as I strived to provide a different conversation on all aspects of money.

Developing and nurturing a positive and meaningful conversation about money through understanding is the basis on which I built and grew my practice. Within these pages, I reveal every element of myself, both personally and professionally, as I share with you all that comprises *Cleopatra's Riches*. This book is the culmination of every aspect of my being, including my connection to my origins in Ancient Egypt, to communicate with you in a way that will most likely be eye-opening for you.

The beauty, richness, and wonder of Ancient Egypt is something I've always had an admiration for, along with the intricacy of its history and culture. When I started to become aware of my own cultural background, which can be traced back to that era, I was struck by just how strong the influence of our origins can be. With that extraordinary and rich cultural context in my mind, I began to develop a different perspective about myself. This girl who grew up in a modest home in a small town in Canada, not having the material wealth of those around me, had the riches of influence from the Ancient Egyptians in her blood. Through this connection came an attachment to the stories I would hear, telling me that I was a direct descendant of Cleopatra. As such, I associated positive feelings with my origins, instead of negative feelings of being "different" and standing out among my peers as a child. My heritage was something I was very aware of, and also became something I was very proud of.

With this in mind, it didn't affect me negatively when I grew up and found out that every Egyptian mother tells her daughter that she's a direct descendant of Cleopatra! Because, for me, I had the positive association and connection—and it always represented a ray of sunshine in my life. When I felt that I didn't belong in my surroundings, my heritage became an anchor to my identity, which inspired the format of the material you'll be reading in this book. I wrote this book with the heartfelt desire that you discover and become more of your true self as the conversation on money becomes the most approachable topic of all—the one in which you are the subject-matter expert, and the author of *your* money story.

Your money story has a rich history that traces back through the generations that preceded you. As a result of my own roots, Egypt is not only at the heart of this book, but at the heart of me as a person. Just as the Nile River was the center of the Ancient Egyptian civilization, so is money as it flows upstream through your life from the moment you were born, until the present day, and throughout your life.

Creating a strong and meaningful understanding of our views, feelings, and beliefs about money is one of the greatest opportunities we have. Until today, when this conversation about money has begun, you probably haven't had a chance to fully understand, connect, or reconcile the influences in your life that created your belief systems around money and the management of it. To develop a strong financial understanding, you may have been taught that you must understand the terms, jargon, and language that are used in the "financial world," instead of directing your focus toward what is most important—an understanding of yourself.

Until now, you've probably been directing your attention toward everything external, giving it priority, and letting it into your life without a true sense of what you've been doing. Through this unconscious habit, you find yourself being dragged down by avoidance—a very powerful form of negativity. In one way or another, you may be avoiding some or many things about your financial picture. What I'm suggesting here is that the reason you're avoiding the money discussion isn't because of a lack of knowledge around definitions, as that's not where financial empowerment comes from. True financial empowerment comes from within.

When you take a step back to do the work in developing a deeper understanding of yourself and the perspective that you're coming from, you'll change your focus from understanding *terms* to understanding *yourself.* The focus of financial information shifts to how it applies to you and its relevance in your life, because you now see yourself at the center of the conversation. This happens by establishing and nurturing a positive relationship with money. To do so, you must develop a clear understanding of each aspect of your money situation in its current state and see how it came to be. This is how to develop a perspective on the Make-Spend Cycle.

MAKE-SPEND CYCLE

Making money and spending it is a cycle most people find themselves in. This cycle is represented in so many different ways in our lives that we haven't had an opportunity to understand it up till now. Let's break this down for a clearer picture of what the words *make* and *spend* represent, and the ways in which they're reflected in our lives, individually and together.

You can make money doing *anything*. Just look around you right now and you'll see money being made at all levels and income brackets. The phrase *making money* commonly represents a disconnect with how money actually comes into your life. The feeling behind *making money* can represent negative feelings such as obligation, guilt, or even greed. In addition, there may be a feeling or belief that there's simply never enough of it. When talking about the money you bring in, the question truly is, What is the *meaning* behind it?

The words we choose have power and influence. When we say "making money," we likely haven't paused to understand the feeling and belief behind it and how we came to form that association. There are so many words and phrases that we use that we're just so accustomed to saying and yet think nothing of it. It's when we pause, for even a moment, to connect to the meaning of those words that it all starts to come together with perspective and an awareness that we didn't have before. As a result, we develop an understanding of what we say and think, the feeling behind it, and what that ultimately represents in what we see—that is, our results.

To better understand this, I will illustrate it with an example relating to one of my very favorite beverages: coffee. If you made a pot of coffee and you spilled some, would it really matter? You'll just make more coffee. The difference here comes from the way you felt about the coffee and its meaning to you. Let's say that the coffee was special to you because it had a positive meaning—maybe it was a gift or a treat. In that case, the positive association creates a very different feeling and associated result (that is, a disappointment when the coffee is spilled, or a feeling that you've lost something valuable that can't just be replaced). It's a positive meaning that causes you to appreciate, value, and enjoy the coffee more because it represents something more.

Let's continue this thought process by reflecting on the feeling behind spending money. Just as is the case with making money, if you look around, you'll find that all kinds of money is being spent. Now, bring that observation internally to you, and you'll find that you can go and spend your money on absolutely anything and for any number of reasons. The key is the feeling *behind* it all. When it comes to spending money, the associated feelings are often negative. It's a matter of choice, and the path to get to that choice begins with a feeling. From here, the question becomes, what *value* was placed on that money that touched and left your hands, and is it being *enjoyed*? The thing is, you may not have been taught to connect to your feelings around money—and if you have, there's likely been a focus on the negative feelings, causing you to lock them away.

In each of those examples, there was a different feeling, meaning, and belief that came together to create a different result. The same concept applies to the way money comes into your life and the way you allocate your expenditures. When you connect to the meaning and feeling of *earning* money, every emotion and resulting decision that follows is different because it all started in the right place.

So, now here we are with making and spending money being associated with negative feelings—but two negatives don't make a positive. The thing is that while we may want change, we find ourselves in a constant loop of the Make-Spend Cycle, where we make money and sometimes it leaves even quicker than it comes in. The challenge is that in so many ways we want to change but don't know how to do so because in one way or another, we keep getting the same results.

MAKE-SPEND-SAVE CYCLE

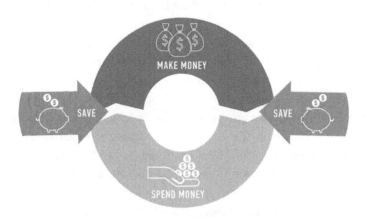

So, in an effort to change, we start to implement what we've been taught to do—save money. On either side of the Make-Spend Cycle, we can try to implement the concept of saving—except that the idea of saving doesn't represent a positive feeling either. So often, it represents a feeling of fear, lack, and scarcity. In addition, we can end up resenting the concept of saving because it's taking away from what we can spend. None of this is positive, so here we are, caught in a negative loop and feeling like there's no way out.

But I'm here to tell you that there *is* a way out! To implement real and lasting change, we must implement something different, and it must start in the right place. We've continued to try to change our negatives with simply another negative, landing us in the same negative loop through all of our external influences.

What we will do here is create real change by connecting to your money story that has developed over the stages of your life, each reflecting its own influences and experiences.

The ideas, feelings, and beliefs related to making, spending, and saving money have been formed over time, not overnight. It's not only all you've been taught, it's what has continually been reinforced on many levels. To have the change that you want, you must unlearn the negative associations you have with making, spending, and saving money in order to relearn and implement the positive associations with earning, growing, and enjoying money.

You see, the feeling behind the words *earn*, *grow*, and *enjoy* are very different. There's a positive association, and it stems from a positive starting place. Essentially, you must unlearn the old Make-Spend Cycle and move toward the new Earn-Grow-Enjoy Model, and the only way you can do that is to understand what you learned in the first place. To do so, you will learn about yourself, one stage of your story at a time. You will also see yourself through the perspective of your experiences and influences.

Developing a conscious awareness through understanding is what you need in order to create the positive changes you desire. That is what this book is about: seeing your perspective in order to make choices that serve, uplift, and move you forward toward the outcomes you're searching for. That search is based on the layers of your financial experiences. No one knows or understands you better than you do, and all we're doing here is talking about you through your story. *You* are the most approachable topic there could be because *you* are the subject-matter expert. That is the mind-set that I ask you to connect with—you being the expert in the study of *you*.

Without the opportunity to develop a comprehensive understanding of our experiences, we often take a one-dimensional view of money. Let's visualize this by "traveling" to the hot desert surrounding the Great Pyramid of Giza in Egypt. As you stand from afar, squinting to protect your eyes from the hot sun and blowing sand, the structure seems one-dimensional. But as you walk through the desert sand to get a closer look, you find that you've walked on a bit of an angle and have taken a few steps to one side, granting you a different perspective of the pyramid. All of a sudden, you see that it isn't the flat triangle it once appeared to be. Wanting to learn and experience more, you walk closer and see that this isn't a simple structure at all, but rather a complicated one constructed of many layers, built one stone at a time. Examining it even closer, you gain an appreciation of the fact that each stone is multidimensional in and of itself. From a distance, the pyramid looked like a simple triangle; however, with a change in perspective, you realize it's actually a very complex structure.

Our relationship with money is equally intricate and complex, but with a change of perspective, we can start to alter that relationship.

PYRAMID OF FINANCIAL INFLUENCES

Through the step-by-step process that I will outline and guide you through within these pages, you will be able to make a positive shift in your feelings and beliefs as you earn, grow, and enjoy your money in the way that you want, and with the balance that you will continue to create. You will build a perspective about your money story as you walk through

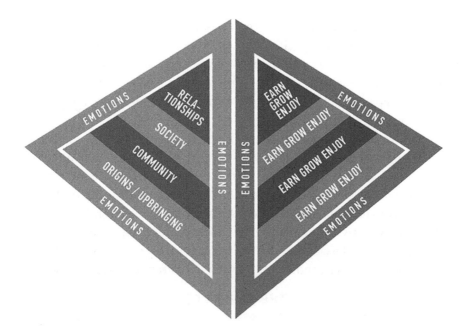

each layer of your own Pyramid of Financial Influences. Your money story developed over time, and so did your beliefs around every aspect relating to money. This is why this conversation will progress in an approachable manner, with each layer and its influences on the way you Earn, Grow, and Enjoy being built purposefully before continuing to the next layer. I have designed this book to be a study of *your* story, influences, and experiences, one layer at a time.

Your story starts with where it all began: your origins. You will walk through a history of your family upbringing, creating a foundational layer upon which everything else is built. From there, you'll move to understanding the aspects surrounding the community you grew up in, and then gain perspective on the societal influences that became hidden in the messages you internalized without realizing it. At this point, you'll then examine your committed relationships and see that these views are what you brought with you before even fully understanding them yourself—which created unspoken and indirect expectations.

By practicing the technique of reframing your thoughts, you're able to regain power over the past, and change the way it affects your thought process in the present. Every "truth" you hold about money carries an associated mind-set, so it's up to you to choose your interpretation: negative or positive. As you dig down deep to uncover the elements of those past experiences and their connected emotions, you'll begin to find the treasures in those experiences, specifically as it relates to your relationship with money. When you acknowledge all of the different sides of your influences, you'll begin to see things more clearly and will be able to move forward with a deeper and more meaningful sense of self and connection to your inner power.

Your experiences and influences brought you to where you are today, but you get to choose *where you're going*. You can choose to be defeated by your experiences or enriched by them. In order to make a meaningful choice, you need to evaluate everything that you're choosing from, and then you can determine the elements that serve, uplift, and push you forward. A positive mind-set allows you to continue to build an appreciation for your experiences and the circumstances of them. Focusing on the word appreciation allows you to give more positive value and meaning to your memories.

THE 4R PROCESS

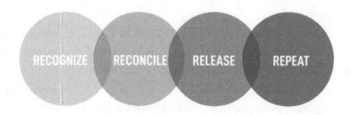

As we continue to delve into this topic, I will ask you to focus on your feelings by seeing, understanding, and then choosing what you appreciate, and work to release what no longer serves you. To do so, I've developed a process for you that I refer to as the "4R Process" of *recognize*, *reconcile*, *release*, and *repeat* the positive. As you travel through the layers of your Pyramid of Financial Influences, you will undoubtedly come to some realizations about your experiences and the associated feelings. From here, with the perspective that you've gained, you will be able to reconcile how those feelings came to be. Then, you can release those negative feelings and associations with gratitude for what you've learned in the process. With this release of the negative, you're implementing the power of your choice as you change the association of that memory or experience to the positive.

It's through the 4R Process that you develop an understanding of your feelings and utilize the power of your choices to create the renewed positive association—emotionalizing to the positive by creating and repeating the positive emotional connection. Now comes the most powerful element, which is to repeat the positive in order to bring the meaningful and lasting change you desire by creating and nurturing a new, positive belief.

You picked up this book for a reason. Perhaps you're searching for something different, pursuing something new, or looking for a missing piece in your life. Here, we will embrace every aspect of money in order to effect the genuine, meaningful, and comprehensive change that you desire. Whatever your reasons may be, it's within your journey through *Cleopatra's Riches* that you will find it, because as you read this book, you will find the answers to the questions you have within you. The only prerequisite is that you *want* to.

When you invested in this book, you invested in yourself. The key to an investment is for it to generate a return for you. Generally, when it comes to investing your money, and even your time, in some way or another you're leaving that return to outside forces.

In this book, I offer you something different—a limitless return. I wrote this so that you could exceed your expectations in every way—and that is exactly what I'm going to show you how to do. I will share with you aspects of who I am so that you can unlock and discover more of who you are, and become more of what you want, in the way that you want.

I am investing my energy in you because I believe in you and your limitless potential. I am investing this time in you because I see you and I *believe* in you. All I ask is that you do the same.

Chapter 1

Origins and Upbringing

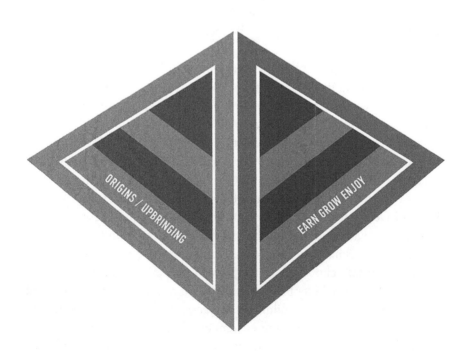

*If you do good to a hundred men and one of them
acknowledges it, no part of it is lost.*

—Egyptian Proverb

We're all storytellers at heart, so when we're asked to talk about our childhood experiences, it's easy to imagine a flood of memories pouring to the surface—significant events and memories that left a lasting impression, and the faces of the people who influenced our lives. These are the stories that contributed to creating the foundation of the individuals we are today. But when most of us think about our pasts and the stories of our upbringing, we default to the facts, especially when we start the conversation around our money stories.

If asked, "What was it like for you growing up?" your natural response may be something like, "My mom worked two jobs and still struggled to make ends meet," or "My parents both had good jobs, so we never had to worry about money," or any number of scenarios in between. But where are *you* in those statements? What did it feel like for *you*? What emotions do you carry with you about those experiences? And most important, where is your perspective? The area where you start to bring positive change comes through seeing yourself in a way you hadn't before. Without that positive connection to your money story, the natural response is to start to look outside of yourself for the direction. The foundation for that positive change is here—in your origins and upbringing.

It's easy to talk about the facts of your upbringing, and it also seems easy to make direct links between where you are in your life today and the circumstances of your childhood. In fact, it's a cliché in pop culture to "blame your parents" for all your current challenges. What you're not used to talking about is your own perspective when it comes to your upbringing. The natural habit is to tell stories from a matter of fact—the details, chronological events, and characters in the story. But when asked to recount your perspective, you may be at a loss for words. You've lost yourself, and as a result have become a secondary character in your own life story. And like the pyramids themselves, the stories you tell are created from individual building stones, each multidimensional in and of themselves. It's when you change your perspective that the distant triangle reveals itself as a beautifully complex pyramid. When you bring awareness to the perspective you have of your own money story, you realize it's no longer a one-dimensional set of facts, but rather a multilayered, multidimensional journey with you at the center.

The ultimate goal when you're talking about starting your money story from the foundation of your origins and upbringing is to recognize where your feelings about money came from in the first place, and to reconcile those feelings as something that no longer serves you, and release them with gratitude because of the lessons you've learned (and then repeat the process as you work toward what I call "emotionalizing your experiences to the positive"). This is the 4R Process that I introduced you to earlier: recognize, reconcile, release, and repeat the positive. We're going to start this process here in the context of your origins and upbringing because this layer truly is the foundation for everything in your life. This process is at the heart of what we're talking about throughout this book, and we're going to be repeating it consistently as we move through the layers of your Pyramid of Financial Influences.

It's through releasing the negative emotions you've associated with money and finances that you'll be able to tap into one of the most positive emotions of all: empathy. You will discover empathy for the characters in your story, and most important, empathy for yourself. When you can see yourself with the perspective of empathy and combine that with your commitment to move forward, you'll be able to knock down the barriers that are currently limiting your financial success. It's also important to note that this release needs to come from a place of gratitude for what you learned. This skill will propel you forward in your results from our conversations, and in so much of your life. This is a simple process that isn't easy, but with a little practice it will be life-changing. When you're stuck in a cycle of negativity, you'll never be able to move forward. Breaking the negative cycle by changing your perspective to the positive will be your gateway to earning, growing, and enjoying your money in the ways you want because you will see yourself for who you are.

At the core of what we're going to be discussing throughout this book is releasing the external influences of your life and turning inward to tap into who you are on the inside. This conversation needs to start by thinking about your upbringing, because this is where the external influences started to inform you, especially when it comes to your view on finances, money, and success.

The vast majority of us will have had little to no exposure to a positive conversation around money in our upbringing. The layer upon layer of negative messaging we received around money and finances carries with us from those first early interactions to the present day, and will therefore become a limiting factor in earning, growing, and enjoying the kind of money we want, in the way that we want.

It's time to unlearn the negative messages that have been weighing you down. Now is the opportunity to become more of yourself as you break the negative money cycle, thereby breaking free from all the barriers that are holding you back. And it needs to start from within *you*. This change can't come from external forces. It has to start with seeing yourself. And the first step in doing so is to change your perspective, which begins by recognizing and appreciating that you have the power to choose how you see things (in other words, you can choose your own perspective). As you work through this chapter (and beyond), I encourage you to think about your own experiences, and connect to how it feels for you. Don't let yourself get lost in the facts. Work through the 4R Process to ultimately change your perspective to focus on emotionalizing those experiences to the positive. Your emotions are completely unique to you. No one can feel the same way you do, so by focusing on your emotions rather than external details, you'll find success in seeing yourself at the center of your own story.

INTRODUCTION TO YOUR ORIGINS

The interactions you had with those who were a part of your childhood household can have the greatest influence over your present-day self because they created the foundation for your beliefs about yourself and the world around you. But in order to better understand where your system of beliefs came from, you must look to the past and determine where the roots of those beliefs stemmed from—your family tree. By going back to the source of those beliefs, you will then have a better chance of determining if those beliefs are serving you, or whether it's time to release them with gratitude. Taking a trip through the past generations in your family tree and thinking about the people and circumstances that shaped your ancestors will shed some light on where you are in your thought process today. This exercise is especially important as part of the conversation around money, since stories of feast and famine are so impactful that they can change the entire direction of a family for many, many generations.

The way your parents interacted with you is a direct reflection of how *their* parents interacted with them, and so on and so on for generations. That's not to say that they copied their own upbringing. Maybe they did, or maybe they were rebelling against it, but either way, the manner in which they raised you was rooted in their own past experiences. Take a moment to recall events or situations that may have particularly impacted one of your relatives, and then think about the messages and associated emotions that may have been passed down because of them.

For a family with Irish roots, the Potato Famine of 1845—even though it only lasted for five years—can still be felt in the present day. The fear, worry, and risk of scarcity could very well still be alive because of the stories that have been passed down for the last eight or nine generations. Humans are storytellers by nature, and family members retell the stories they heard from their parents, which could make the fear around the famine feel very real if those are the stories you've been told. Through the telling and retelling of that family story, those here in the 21st century could be internalizing the feeling that, at any given moment, famine is a real possibility, and therefore are unconsciously preparing for that day in their actions and decisions around how they earn, grow, and enjoy their money.

In North America, scarcity is commonly associated with the immigrant experience, which affects the vast majority of Americans. According to the 2010 Census, less than 2 percent of the current population is indigenous to the land; therefore, a full 98 percent of people will have an immigrant story in their family history. Having the themes of scarcity and struggle streaming through you without any real awareness could have a huge impact on your decisions about the future—with very real financial results.

The topic of money and wealth is not unique to any one culture. Many societies, even today, are influenced by beliefs and superstitions associated with money. While there's nothing innately wrong with superstitions and cultural traditions (in fact, they can provide you with a sense of grounding, pride in your culture, and even a bit of fun), it's still important to bring awareness to those beliefs and the resulting emotions, and then decide if they're serving you and are uplifting or if they're creating barriers that are preventing you from moving forward in your life.

The Ancient Egyptians had a very strong system of beliefs that we can still see in popular Egyptian culture today. A specific example of this is the concept of the Evil Eye, which is the belief that another person can bring negativity or evil into one's life with just one jealous glance. Belief in the power of the Evil Eye was something I was consistently exposed to in my upbringing because it exists in my origin. This is a particularly poignant example because in the superstition of the Evil Eye, we're giving another person control over us by believing that their gaze, or jealous thought, can actually have a meaningful impact on our lives. If we internalize the emotions associated with the fear of jealousy because of what we were told growing up, then we're actively allowing them to control our decisions. Without an understanding of where these beliefs came from, I could have easily taken the Evil Eye concept at face value.

This is a very concrete example of how external influences can affect us in a profound way. When there's a belief in the power of someone's jealousy, major decisions around earning, growing, and enjoying money can change or become limited (in the case of the Egyptians, to avoid the Evil Eye). Now, with that in mind, it becomes very obvious how a belief like this may limit someone's financial situation, future growth potential, and overall enjoyment of one's hard-earned money.

This is just one example of how your origins can have a direct impact on your financial situation today. Your finances aren't separate from who you are and how you came to be this person—they are one and the same story. Knowing where a particular idea came from and the path it took to get to you puts you in a better position to make an informed decision as to whether to accept it or reject it (or in other words, *recognize* the belief, *reconcile* if it's serving you, *release* it with gratitude for what you've learned, and *repeat* the process).

That choice to release a belief that is no longer serving to uplift you helps to create the richness of your self-identity. This is an important point because we so often segregate money from our journey of self-identity. But in reality, money is woven throughout the influences that make us who we are. When we eliminate money from the conversation, we eliminate a part of ourselves. So in our journey of self-discovery, it's imperative that we include the influences of money. Our relationship with money is a part of who we are, and once we make the decision to approach it as a positive part of our emotions and thinking, we take off the limiters we've placed on ourselves. When we *see* ourselves, we can *be* ourselves. If we really want to see clearly, we need to see the whole picture, and that starts in our origins. Once we have a handle on the foundation of who we are, we can narrow the scope to the elements that have had a direct impact, or more specifically, our upbringing.

INTRODUCTION TO YOUR UPBRINGING

Now that you've taken a wide-angled view of your heritage and created a historical context for your system of beliefs, you can narrow your thought process down to your own experiences in childhood. Keeping your perspective at the top of your mind, you can begin to understand how your upbringing shaped your current situation as it relates to money. This self-reflection is a huge missing piece in most financial conversations. Money is so often tied up with negative feelings—shame, embarrassment, guilt, envy, obligation, just to name a few—and it's most likely that you'll find that the roots of those emotions lie somewhere in the messaging you received about money in your childhood. With an understanding of your roots, you'll also have a more solid basis for understanding your parents and where their perspectives on money and success came from—maybe with an added layer of empathy for them, and ultimately, yourself.

Whether your parents were in stable careers, were entrepreneurs, or were working paycheck to paycheck, I'm sure you overheard the conversations about rent or mortgage payments, household bills, pay freezes at work, impending economic slowdowns, or the ebbs and flows that come from running a family business. Maybe your young brain didn't understand what all of this meant, but you certainly understood that there were things you couldn't do or have because of your family's financial situation. And you could probably also sense the stress, anxiety, and negativity around those money conversations.

Growing up in an immigrant family, I felt strongly that I didn't truly belong in my Egyptian culture, but I felt equally displaced in my immediate environment (a small, affluent town in Canada). Born in Egypt during a time of prosperity, my parents were affected by the political turmoil at that time in such a way that leaving everything behind to come to Canada for a better life was the most reasonable option. This experience affected my parents deeply and helped form their perspective on many areas of life, including their financial situation and the messaging they passed along to their children.

One message I recognized from my childhood—and one that I've had to do my own work to *recognize*, *reconcile*, and *release*—relates to discussions around my career path. My parents' messaging was very clear to my sister and me: do well in school, go to a respected university, and land yourself a good career. But where the context of my culture started to creep in is in what constituted a "good career." My parents made it very clear— directly and indirectly—that the acceptable career paths were doctor, dentist, pharmacist, or engineer. The only slight deviation from this list was a government job with a good pension. I lovingly term these the "fab five" career paths. Basically, if your child chose one of the "fab five" careers, then you'd made it as a parent. It was really difficult for me to tell my parents that I didn't want to pursue any of their approved career paths. My decision-making process could have easily come from a place of guilt, fear, or obligation, and those feelings are very often the driving force behind major life decisions for many people.

The influences of your family go beyond the household you were raised in and the immediate family that surrounded you. Your extended family—grandparents, aunts, uncles, cousins, and so on—can also have an emotional impact on your beliefs around money, even if they weren't a part of your day-to-day life. Your extended family can make their mark on your experiences and feelings around money in many different ways because they were part of your parents' upbringing. Although relationships with extended family members can be complex, money can certainly be a contributing factor, and in some instances, the single element that either keeps everyone connected or creates a great divide.

As I'm recounting my own experiences here for you, memories from your own childhood will probably be flooding back. What I want you to do is use these triggers to start thinking about your own experiences and the messaging you received from inside your childhood household and recognize the emotions associated with those experiences. Start to think about your perspective. And as you do so, ask yourself: "What is another way that I can look at this?" With a better understanding of who you are and where you came from, can you start to feel more empathy toward the characters in your story—especially toward yourself?

My childhood wasn't easy, but I've done the work to change my perspective using the 4R Process to reevaluate the negative experiences and choose a positive perspective. This focus away from the negative is what I referred to earlier as "emotionalizing to the positive." I made the conscious decision not to drown in my own negative emotions, but rather to change my perspective on these situations, and recognize that all of these messages from my upbringing came from a place of love.

When *you* are able to focus on the positive feelings associated with your upbringing, then you'll be able to remove the barriers that are holding you back from moving forward in your life and your financial situation.

Chapter 2

How Origins and Upbringing Affect Earning Money

*It is better to dwell in your small house than to
dwell in the large house of another.*

—Egyptian Proverb

Time management, conflict resolution, and resiliency are the essential soft skills that will make you a valuable income earner. The foundation for these skills was shaped inside your household. The values that you were raised with and the experiences you had at home also prepared you for life in the "real world," so to speak. The pressure that parents feel to raise their children to be both happy and productive could fill an entire book—in fact, *many, many* books (just go to your local bookstore and see for yourself). As you move through childhood, the conversation switches from passive skill-building exercises to a hard look at what you want to do for the rest of your life. Whether or not you choose to actively participate in that conversation, the seeds have been planted, letting you know that how you earn money is a high priority.

There are so many different ways in which your origins and upbringing can influence or even direct your career path. Even more so, it can impact your feelings and beliefs about yourself and your abilities, defining or limiting your self-worth. Just look at the factors in your present circumstances and you'll be able to see how messages or influences from your upbringing are reflected in your current life. This thought process may bring positive feelings, negative feelings, and everything in between. What you're doing here is building an awareness of your present-day results as they relate to your upbringing.

At this point in your timeline, the main frame of reference that you have for what earning money looks like comes from your household. How your family members make (or made) money and the relationship they have with that money has a vital impact on what you're going to pursue, because you have an emotional connection with that messaging. Your future employment could be based on necessity, for any number of reasons, or a conscious decision to follow in your parents' footsteps… or a conscious decision not to.

At the root of what you do to earn money is your upbringing—and by extension, your origins. This can be a significant contributor to the idea of making money as opposed to earning it because you often make decisions based on what you know—what's familiar and comfortable. Your upbringing can be comfortable as far as the familiar careers, jobs, or businesses that your parents were in, and perhaps their parents before them. This isn't to say that if you're in the same or a similar career as your parents that you cannot be happy—that's simply not true. Instead, my point here is to illustrate the underlying feelings behind your career decision. Did it come from a positive place within you, or a negative place outside of you? Were you seeking guidance about your decision, or were you following someone else's direction? There are so many examples and scenarios that could stem from your upbringing. Taking a step back to evaluate those influences will shed some light on your current situation. If you're not on the career path that you want to be on, you're likely not expressing your skills and abilities, which is preventing you from earning money in the way you want.

Looking to my upbringing, when I view my career path from the perspective of my parents and the influence from their culture, the business degree I obtained just doesn't carry the same value as a path in medicine or science, as mentioned earlier in this chapter. Because I chose to deviate from my parents' wishes, they constantly expressed their concern for my future and long-term earning potential. Their deeply rooted cultural values had provided them with a very narrow view on what was best for me. Family dynamics and expectations often play a huge role in choosing a particular path. I certainly could have pursued one of their approved careers simply out of feelings of guilt or obligation. The way our families view, prioritize, and encourage certain career paths matters, and to go against that influence is more difficult than we may realize.

Just look to your own circle of peers and you will undoubtedly see how often people tend to gravitate toward the careers of their parents or other close family members. In many cases, we start our careers in something that is approved of or encouraged by our parents because that's what they know from their experience, and by extension, that's what *we* know.

When asking yourself these questions, you're applying your parents' perspective to your experience. Maybe they encouraged you to choose something different because they've experienced hardships associated with their job choices or opportunities. Or on the flip side, maybe they've seen great success and hope that their children will experience the same. There's nothing innately negative about either path. The key to earning the money you want comes from knowing yourself and having a connection to your gifts, preferences, and abilities from a place of positivity and appreciation.

Many of you may not be connected to your purpose because you're lost in someone else's vision. Maybe that vision comes from something intangible and uncontrollable, like your origin or upbringing, but what you can control is how you perceive those intangibles. If your overriding emotions around earning money are negative, chances are that no matter how much of it you make, your resulting emotions will be negative, therefore limiting your growth and ultimate potential. It's through the practice of the 4R Process of *r*ecognizing, *r*econciling, *r*eleasing, and *r*epeating the positive that you're tapping into and unlocking what's behind the barriers you've created for yourself.

Chapter 3

How Origins and Upbringing Affect Growing Money

Wealth and saving are the equal of work.

—Egyptian Proverb

On the surface, the Earn-Grow-Enjoy Model, as mentioned in the intro-duction, fits quite nicely into the context of origins and upbringing. Without too much thought, it's easy to see how your family background influences your ideas around how to *earn* money. It's also fairly obvious that the same experiences would have influenced how you *enjoy* money. So by extension, how you *grow* your money would also have an obvious connec-tion. You'd think so, but the reality is that for the vast majority of people, their parents fell short on communicating a system for growing money.

Most of us saw firsthand what our parents did to earn money. They worked. And they talked about working. Even if we weren't directly involved in those conversations, we had knowledge of them and internalized the resulting emotions. We also saw the enjoyment they got from spending the money they earned—or on the flip side, we understood what it was like when they didn't have money to enjoy. And even if money wasn't available for "enjoyment," we still had a sense of what enjoying money could look like.

From a young age, we were intimate participants in the home economics of making money and then spending it. But right there is the exact problem: Where's the "grow" in that model? At a very basic level, we all have a context for discussing earning and enjoying, but most of us are missing the same context for growing. We feel a connection with earn and enjoy because they were both regular occurrences in our childhood that we created very strong emotional ties to. But when it comes to growing money, there's the missing piece of the puzzle.

We have a distance from it stemming from our childhood, because as children we had more of a connection to the instant gratification of earning and enjoying. Growing is a slow process, and for so many, even the idea of "saving" brings up negative feelings. For example, if there is a savings plan in place, parents may feel the need to shield their children from it for fear of cultivating feelings of greed or entitlement. If there are no savings, that's information they may not wish to share with their children. As a result, we grow up without a context in which to form an understanding of how to grow the money we earn.

Investments, retirement plans, and savings accounts seem like issues for our future selves to worry about. If your parents do have savings, you may only see it once they hit the retirement years, and then all of a sudden there's a pool of capital that seems to have simply appeared—that is, a pension, 401(k), or other investments. We may have had no exposure to, or understanding of, the accumulation stage, so essentially there's no in between. No one taught us how to grow our money. As we reach adulthood, there's just an expectation that we know what we're doing with the money we're making. But, of course, that's not necessarily true.

The idea of saving your money may hold a negative connotation because of its connection to scarcity—especially if you have a cultural connection to it in your origins or are living it in your upbringing. The term *squirrelling away* is often a synonym for *savings*. Creating a saving account can be directly tied to the idea of putting money away for an impending disaster (just as a squirrel gathers nuts for the impending season of scarcity—that is, winter). That's a very discouraging way to view savings. Naturally, we want to think about things that make us happy, not things that bring up feelings of stress and worry. Creating savings often brings up emotions such as stress and worry, whereas spending money brings up happy feelings associated with instant gratification.

To move forward, we need to acknowledge the feelings holding us back from growing our money, and take control by removing the barriers that are holding us back. We need to shift our perspective from that of negativity to a judgment-free place of understanding. It's easy to see why we gravitate more toward conversations around earning and enjoying, and actively avoid that you really can't speak about one without involving the others, and if you're simply ignoring a large piece of the puzzle, you may feel like things just aren't falling into place. Through realizing your feelings and experience (or lack thereof) on growing money, you can reconcile the reasons why, release the negative, and begin repeating the positive by shifting to an active role.

As we continue these conversations in future chapters, I'll discuss the concept of growing more.

Chapter 4

How Origins and Upbringing Affect Enjoying Money

Whether times are strait or joyous, wealth grows by spreading it.

—Egyptian Proverb

As we've already established, what you observed about your parents, family, culture, and the way in which money was enjoyed can be strongly linked to what you believe enjoying money means to you. But let's explore this idea further and gain some perspective on the issue of how to enjoy your money, because it may not be as straightforward as you think.

If your parents were frugal when you were growing up, you may now have a tendency to go toward the opposite extreme, where enjoyment from spending money becomes a priority. This type of "rebellion" can lead some down the path of debt, which is obviously not an ideal situation within the context of this conversation. And on the opposite extreme, if you grew up with an example of excessive spending and witnessed the debt and stress that resulted from that, you may be inclined to derive little enjoyment from your money because of the negative feelings you've internalized—that is, enjoying your money equals stress or guilt. This can be equally problematic because enjoyment is a critical part of living a balanced life, and, as I mentioned earlier, enjoying money is not the same as spending. Enjoying money comes from a place of positivity, whereas spending money comes from a negative place.

One of the most influential and positive messages I received from my parents was the belief that the gift of giving is directly linked to enjoyment. My parents weren't considered materially wealthy, but they always gave whatever they could—both with time and money—to help charities and organizations they had a connection to. They truly modeled that enjoyment of money isn't necessarily linked to buying things.

There's a particular example that has really stuck with me, even to this day. We would regularly put aside the clothes that no longer fit us so they could be donated, and when my dad would travel to Egypt to visit family, he would take these items and pass them along to charities in his home-town. He wanted my sister and me to understand what he was experiencing during his travels, so he would diligently pack his camcorder and bring back VHS tapes full of video footage.

On one particular recording, he had captured some images of a Sunday-school classroom filled with children around my own age. I immediately focused my attention on these images because of the instant connection I felt with these kids—they were not only my age, but they *looked* like me. The camera panned around the classroom, and my eye was drawn to a young girl who was wearing the same dress that I had worn the previous Easter. Suddenly, my donation was no longer theoretical; it was right in front of my eyes. In that moment, I created a positive emotional attachment to giving to others. I knew how happy that dress had made me, and now I was witnessing someone else enjoying it and feeling equally happy. Throughout my childhood, I would continue to witness my parents' acts of selflessness.

And I've manifested this lesson through my own career by linking the positive emotions of enjoying money with the gift of giving. In more than one way, managing your money can lead to greater enjoyment. If giving is something that you want to do, you can do more of it by making the decision from a place of openness and positivity. Money becomes an amplifier for the good that you want to create. It is directly through my parents' dedication to giving back that I understand the joy associated with humility, love, and service.

Part of truly enjoying your money comes with creating a balance. And that balance comes from knowing yourself and what you want. Giving will not provide you with enjoyment if the motivation doesn't come from within you. If you're giving money out of obligation, that's spending it, not enjoying it. The messaging I took from my parents and the fact that I chose to focus on the positive associated emotions impact how I choose to earn and grow my money, thereby creating the balance I want.

Often, an imbalance in the Earn-Grow-Enjoy Model stems from negative associations and unmatched ideas and expectations in our upbringing. To move forward, we need to release the negativity with gratitude, and be happy about what we have learned from it. It's not the process of just saying, "I'm over it." It's more about the way you release those emotions. Feeling connected to these decisions with empathy for the situation will help get you to a place of true release.

Chapter 5

Community

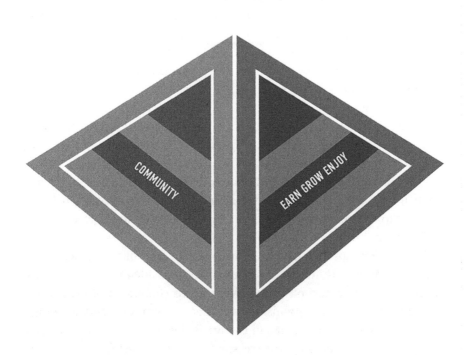

He who loves his neighbor finds family around him.

—Egyptian Proverb

Up until this point of your storyline, the focus has been inside your childhood home. You've looked at your origin story, those who played a role in your upbringing, and how those early influences began to shape your Earn-Grow-Enjoy Model. But as you grew up, you started having more experiences outside of your home. It's these experiences in the broader community where you began to realize that there's an entire world of influences out there. Therefore, the next layer of your Pyramid of Financial Influences must be the community. It's when you see yourself as a member of the broader outside world that you start to receive new information. And it's this new information that is going to either support or contrast the ideas and messaging that you've received from your origins and upbringing.

When we're talking about community, we're looking at places, situations, and organizations such as schools, religious or spiritual centers, sports teams, arts and cultural opportunities, and parks or other communal gathering spaces—basically anything that goes into bringing people together based on their location. In each of these elements of the community, you're being exposed to different people and ideas that are helping to shape your own belief system.

These subgroups each have their own individual set of beliefs, behaviors, and expectations. Think back to the schools you attended, to the dance studios you were a part of, or the sports teams you played on—each one was like a little community inside itself. Each community, and subgroup, has its own set of beliefs that can essentially become hidden within your thought processes because they're supported by so many other people around you. In the book *Group Psychology and the Analysis of the Ego*, Sigmund Freud attempted to understand how an individual's behavior, thoughts, and emotions are affected when they become part of a group. A key point in this work is that people naturally seek to be a part of various groups to feel safe; however, with this feeling of belonging often comes a loss of your own conscious thoughts, emotions, and desires.

Now, there's nothing wrong with being influenced by your community—in fact, involvement with different aspects of your community can add an unparalleled richness to your life. But if you leave those influences unexplored, you can find yourself limited by them rather than uplifted.

When it comes to money, you may not have positive feelings around the topic because you haven't been exposed to an example of positivity. If all you saw were negative messages around money in your home and among the community groups you were a part of, you may not have the tools to change the conversation on your own. It's through the process of identifying those early influences and implementing the 4R Process that will equip you with the tools to emotionalize your finances to the positive.

Both expectation and perception come into play here as well. As you read about how your community has affected your beliefs and feelings around money, think about what you believed the people around you expected of you. Then consider how those beliefs made you feel and the impact they had. Growing up in a specific area can have a significant impact on what you perceived was expected of you. When it comes to careers, if you grew up in an area where you were expected and encouraged to follow a particular career path, it's likely that's what you're doing. For example, if you grew up in a mining town, you're more likely to be drawn to that career path, or something related. Essentially, you've taken the external expectations, internalized them as your own beliefs, and breathed that into life in your choice of job or career.

The way you believe others perceived you can truly shape your lifelong decisions. This is particularly noticeable in the messages you received as a student. A common example of this would be for someone to have been labeled a "bad student" simply because of behavioral issues or a low GPA. Messaging like that could lead you to believe that you aren't smart and therefore shouldn't pursue college education or that you won't succeed at the trade you wanted to pursue. That internalized perception has now become a very significant limiting factor.

The area where you grew up in can also influence your limiting beliefs as far as what opportunities are available to you. Your community may have essentially created a belief in you that you can only do so much or only be so much simply because of where you came from. On the flip side, there are also examples of how you can feel limited by your community because you believe that you'll never be like the people who are part of it.

This was a belief that I could have easily chosen. In previous chapters, I've touched on the fact that I grew up in an affluent area, but I didn't grow up in an affluent household. And I was consistently reminded that my household was different from those of my peers. These differences were fuel for how much I was teased, ridiculed, and looked down upon by the kids in my surrounding community, especially at school.

My own educational experiences are ones that I reconciled and released in particular when it came to the impact of my peers' perceptions. Being teased or bullied by other children is not a story exclusive to me. These experiences are unfortunately all too common and shared by so many of us. I'm discussing this here because it can be a significant impact on what we internalize, the way we feel, and what we believe about ourselves. So many lies can be internalized about ourselves that have become unnoticed because we were told them so many times that they became true. But these negative beliefs don't have to remain!

In my situation, the teasing was very much linked to money. Growing up in an affluent neighborhood without the material wealth of the kids in the community made me a clear and easy target. I lived with a feeling of being "less than," and the treatment I received from my peers reinforced that feeling for me. I didn't just *feel* less than; I was told that it was a fact. Not wearing the clothes or having the things that they did made me stand out, and at the center of it all was money. For me, the negative feelings associated with the teasing could have easily influenced negative beliefs around money, like the idea that money was associated with the negative behavior I was experiencing. But it didn't, and when I look now to analyze why, the reason was clearly within me.

While being heavily teased, I wanted to find a safe space, and for that I turned inward. In the process of looking within myself, I found that I would protect myself with positive internal messaging, focusing on all the things I loved and that made me who I am. A part of that came from my heritage, which I connected to from a positive place. From within myself I was learning the power of choice, connecting to positive emotions and associations. Every time I was teased, it became another opportunity to practice that skill. That was where I truly began to emotionalize to the positive and become more of myself as a result. It's that skill that I still put into practice every day and that I am sharing with you here.

As I mentioned before, your community can influence your limiting beliefs as far as which opportunities are available to you. After being exposed to very basic business concepts through school, I became fascinated by the topic, and this interest guided my high school experience. I focused solely on this study, but this choice of career paths was discouraged by my parents and the school, because it was perceived as being as too narrow. Their view was that I needed to take a variety of classes to "keep my options open." Their concern was understandable, because by not taking science classes, I was essentially eliminating an entire set of potential career options. I could have focused on negative feelings such as intimidation or judgment, which may have caused me to make a decision out of spite or self-doubt, but the negative emotions would have undoubtedly led to negative results.

When you allow your community to become a limiting factor, it will affect your Earn-Grow-Enjoy Model on every level. Your community can be the starting point of the connection to your passion and purpose. In my own situation, I could have made critical life decisions based on negative feelings and beliefs. Instead, I focused on the positive emotions I felt around my decision, and built the belief that I would be successful in my chosen career. I chose to rise above the negativity and carve out my own path, despite the messaging I was receiving from my community.

You also have a choice. You can allow external forces to affect your decisions around money and finances by accepting what your community told you to expect about your future. Or, you can choose to break through these limitations. It's when you release your limiting beliefs that you're able to choose your inner power and rise up to your true potential.

Chapter 6

How Community Affects Earning Money

The virtue of a wise man is to gather without greed.

—Egyptian Proverb

When talking about how community places limitations on you, the most profound example is in how you earn money. Each institution in your community, whether it's a school, spiritual entity, or other community group, will provide you with messages on what you can and can't do once you leave that community and enter into adulthood. This is especially evident when it comes to messaging around your career path.

Although messaging about careers and earning money starts in the home, it's in the community setting where you're encouraged to start making major life decisions. School is the most obvious example because the job of the school system is to prepare you for your future career path. At this point in your life, you're also used to relying on your parents, so it's natural that you would carry this tendency to look for direction versus guidance when you enter into the school system. With direction, you're focused on external influences telling you where to go. This is part of creating a definition of who you are based on external characteristics. With guidance, however, the focus shifts to amplifying who you already are from the inside.

In elementary school, the system is looking to help you build soft skills and create a basic foundation for knowledge. The idea of direction versus guidance becomes more noticeable in high school as the focus shifts toward developing hard skills for a specific path. The courses you take at this time are intended to point you toward some type of job where you'll earn money. If you're being directed, you can lose connection with what you really want. If you're being guided, who you are on the inside is the main focus; and the courses are serving to enhance those qualities, passions, and talents. As you think back to your own teachers and classmates, you'll be able to identify the times that you were directed and the times that you were guided.

The problem is when you're being directed by an outside influence and that direction actually creates barriers for you, rather than uplifts you in a way that truly exemplifies who you are. On the other hand, when education comes from guidance, you can be connected to your passion and discover your purpose.

This was the case for me when I had my first taste of entrepreneurship in an elementary school class. Due to funding cuts that year, we weren't able to take class trips. But our teacher gave us a choice: we could accept this fate or not. We chose not to. As we began brainstorming ideas of how we could go on our own class trip, I was captivated because she was including us—a bunch of kids—into the conversation. And we were given ownership of the results.

So how did we make it happen? Potato chips. The school didn't sell snacks, so we decided to open a store and sell chips during lunch breaks. It was a win-win. I felt the most myself as I actively listened and contributed to the process. This was perhaps the first time I had a real sense of belonging in my school community. But beyond that, in a very gentle way, I was being introduced to basic business concepts. The bill for the chips was due 30 days after the first order, so I learned about credit. I also saw the concept of supply and demand firsthand as I watched the students line up to buy our product. We did, by the way, earn enough money to take a class trip, but the pride we felt over what we had earned gave our work greater meaning. This is not only an example of how a community can connect us to our passions, but also how an education can provide guidance over direction.

When education is focused on the idea of guidance, not direction, this is when educators are able to add so much value, and why I personally loved being a schoolteacher so much. I have always been committed to applying my belief in guidance in the classroom, and then in my boardroom as a financial professional, and now more than ever as I bring these two areas together in our conversation here.

My experiences as a teacher truly helped me see just how influential community can be. Time and again, I saw students who were so used to being directed that they became completely disconnected with the idea of what they actually wanted. As I'd help guide my students, I'd apply what I call the "magic formula." This formula starts with a "spark" and self-confidence, which leads to a value proposition, and ultimately a definition of success.

Now, take a moment to reflect on what you loved to do when your community was the most influential (beginning around when you started elementary school, until the end of high school, before you got your first job as a young adult). What were your passions? What activities were you most drawn to? What fueled your energy and brought you joy? Then take a moment to remember what you believed you would do for a career at that time. Or, with a little reflection, think about whether there was something you could have seen yourself doing based on those early sparks of joy.

For most of us, there was something we were passionate about or that we were drawn to at that age—a sport or activity; an art form such as dance, painting, or drama; a certain subject in school; a project that really impacted you. These were sparks. And there's a good chance that if you think back, you could have imagined yourself pursuing these sparks as a career path. There's an equally good chance that you expressed this interest to someone in authority (a parent, a teacher, a guidance counselor). What was this person's reaction? "You'll never make money doing that." Or "You can't do that. You won't make enough money." Sound familiar? While the intent is essentially honorable, what is happening is that the community was trying to push you toward something more practical. And, as actor Jim Carrey said during a graduation speech given in 2014 at Maharishi University of Management in Iowa, "So many of us choose our path out of fear disguised as practicality."

The messaging we received from our community created a sense of fear within us. When you internalize that fear, your confidence is decreased and your self-image is negatively affected. You can then begin to question how well you actually know yourself. If your sense of self is in question, the natural reaction is to look outside for a definition of who you really are. A common thought process around this would be something like, "Maybe they *do* know what's best for me." And it's from this place of lacking self-confidence that you started making decisions rooted in a place of negativity. You were then led to believe that you couldn't pursue your passions, and instead took the path toward something more practical. But when a belief about yourself is based on negative emotions—in this example, fear and insecurity—your results are going to be negative as well. And in this case, the results relate to how you earn money and how much you earn.

When you combine your spark and self-confidence to the positive, you're expressing your gifts in the way you want to. The application of this leads you to your definition of success. With this idea, the whole concept started with you and continued with you, because everything was directed from within. This is where guidance serves to uplift you.

When it's broken down like this, it all seems really simple—but the application of this mind-set shift isn't easy, and the reason is because it's not what we've been taught. When we're susceptible to direction, our spark is dampened with the practical or approved career paths we're often directed toward, and our confidence declines with the pressure of fitting in.

It's when you take the opportunity to walk through the layers of your Pyramid of Financial Influences that you can reconnect with your spark. And as you emotionalize that spark to the positive, you'll be able to connect with a more positive belief on how to use those passions, talents, and preferences to enhance your results. Maybe you're following your passions in your current career path, but reconnecting with what brought you here in the first place will remind you of the positive emotions that you were initially connected with. If you didn't follow this path, reconnecting with those passions and changing the emotions toward the positive will also change your belief in who you are on the inside. When you're connected with positive emotions and a positive belief in yourself, this is where the positive results of earning more money begin. If you don't take the time to understand yourself and your emotions, you'll never be able to move forward in your earning potential. What you're doing here is exactly that: taking the time to understand yourself and your emotions in a meaningful way.

Chapter 7

How Community Affects Growing Money

He who does not gather wood in summer will not be warm in winter.

—Egyptian Proverb

When we haven't developed a strong understanding and positive connection with growing money from our familial homes, we tend to look externally for direction. The first place we're exposed to outside of our upbringing is our community. The irony of the situation is that there's this endless loop around who is supposed to teach us how to manage and grow our money. The community expects that you're learning this at home, but there's also the expectation that you're learning it in school. Essentially, no one is taking the responsibility for teaching us these skills, and we're left with no tools or ability to grow our money when the time comes.

If we weren't learning about growing our money at home, then the next logical place to seek understanding is through education. But the majority of us had little to no exposure as far as learning practical financial skills and literacy in school. In a 2018 study published in the *Children and Youth Services Review*, it was reported that nearly a third of young adults surveyed were found to have poor financial literacy and lacked money management skills, directly leading to being categorized as "financially precarious" (in other words, not having a stable income). The fact that we're not being formally taught this type of information can have a significant impact on our thought processes and mind-set because subconsciously we can view it as unimportant.

Let's pause for some perspective of how this lack of exposure can impact one's viewpoint. If you didn't learn about financial matters in a practical way at home, and you didn't learn about it at all in school, then you've basically spent about a quarter of your life without any exposure to, or understanding of, this topic. Then you grow up and feel the pressure of expectation to delve right into "adult life" with essentially no actual knowledge of how to grow your money. Or if you do have a knowledge base, you have to consider whether the messaging was positive or negative—more likely than not it was negative, and it isn't serving you in a productive way.

Growing your money isn't something that is seen unless you have access to the information. You can see people earning money, and you can see people enjoying it, but it's the in-between step that really has no obvious visual cue. How many of us saw the bank statements, financial reports, or income tax filings from anyone around us? So much emphasis is placed on earning and enjoying, but growing just kind of gets lost—out of sight, out of mind.

If we're only focused on the things that others can see, then we can easily lose ourselves in the equation. As a result of my own upbringing in a wealthy area but without the material wealth of my community, I could have a tendency to place greater importance on earning and enjoying money, because that's what would be seen by others as a way to prove that I did actually belong there. If that's what I had chosen, I would be internalizing the opinions or views of others to the negative in my own decisions, which would have only served to limit myself and my potential as a result.

This same decision-making process can take place in many different circumstances. For example, if you grew up in an area that was not considered wealthy and you advanced to a position of success, then you may feel the pressure, obligation, or desire to show everyone just how successful you are. In either thought process, little to no importance is placed on growing money because it's not being seen. Building a positive connection, understanding, and awareness within ourselves allows us to ensure that our decisions are based on our own betterment rather than justification or acceptance.

It's here now that you're breaking free from the cycle of negativity. You're breaking away from the Make-Spend Cycle and are transitioning to the Earn-Grow-Enjoy Model, and you're also breaking the cycle for the next generation. If you have children, or are thinking of having them, empowering yourself means that you'll also be able to empower them through the conversations and messages you teach. Involving them in financial conversations in a positive light allows them to build their own positive emotions that you've laid the foundation for.

As a parent, what I consistently see is that when we make something matter to kids in a positive way, we make it meaningful to them. Changing the conversation around money, especially when it comes to growing it, will need to start at home with individuals, and then it will lead to a trickle effect into the community and beyond.

Chapter 8

How Community Affects Enjoying Money

Poverty does not rule over him who controls himself in expenditure.

—Egyptian Proverb

Often when it comes to enjoying money, our spending habits are based on other people. At the center of those external influences is comparison. The concept of comparison is a large and involved topic in and of itself. It's one that weaves throughout our relationship with money.

You may have felt the weight of comparison on you in your upbringing, but it's really amplified once you begin to explore who you are within your community. One result of comparison could be that enjoying money becomes so strongly connected to the idea of being accepted by those around you that you lose sight of what you really want. If you're basing how you spend money on a comparison with others, you're simply spending money, not enjoying it. There are very few truly positive emotions connected to spending money, which is why it's important to make the shift from spending to enjoying. Basically, it's best not to use money to replace something that's missing or creating something within you that wasn't there.

In the words of Theodore Roosevelt, "Comparison is the thief of joy." If enjoying your money doesn't start from within, you're going to be left with feelings of dissatisfaction. You're also running the risk of spending beyond your means. Enjoying money is about amplifying the positive about yourself that you want to be more of. To do so, you must start connecting with who you are on the inside by blocking out negative external influences. Comparison comes from the outside in, but you want to reverse that and focus on the inside out.

Oftentimes, comparison starts when you venture into your community and see yourself as someone more than just your origins and upbringing. For example, whether it's the intention or not, you're compared in all facets of your education—by your teachers, in extracurricular activities, in standardized testing, by your fellow students, and even with other schools.

When you're exposed to people outside of your home, you also start to notice what you do or do not have in comparison with your neighbors, peers, and the other people around you.

Comparison was most certainly something that I dealt with growing up, feeling different from those around me. I wanted so much to be like them and to look like them. When I was younger, I had the idea that one day I would make enough money to buy the things I didn't have as a kid. I'd wear designer brands. I'd drive the right kind of car. And I would live in a big, fancy house like my classmates did. When I had these things, then I would find the sense of belonging I was searching for. In reality, that goal was coming from a really negative place. Remember the story of my elementary school class selling chips to earn money for a class trip? The trip was an excellent example of how to enjoy money from a place of positivity. The desire for the trip came from us, not anyone else. If someone had told us that we should go on a trip, the results of our project would have been very different.

Over the years, I realized that by focusing on the goal of having what my peers had, I was losing meaning within myself and placing the priority on others. I was depreciating my own value and losing sight of all the wonderful things I was gifted with. I had a great upbringing, in a great area with great schools. I had a loving family for whom I will be forever grateful. And as my thought process shifted to gratitude for what I had, I began to love and appreciate the gifts of my influences and experiences.

In basing my spending on others, I was confusing inspiration with comparison. I thought I was being inspired by those around me, but in fact I was comparing myself to them. When we compare ourselves to others, we're giving control to the other person or group, and in the process, we're losing ourselves. Comparison is a negative lens in which we criticize and demean ourselves. Inspiration, however, is a positive lens filled with gratitude for who we are with a desire to grow and improve. Spending is based on comparison and is connected to negative feelings, whereas enjoying money based on inspiration is emotionalizing to the positive. As a result, being inspired actually encourages us to become more of ourselves through an uplifting set of thoughts. Comparison and inspiration are two sides of the same coin—it's *your* choice as to what side your thought process is landing on.

The community you grew up in can also have a significant impact on the way you enjoy money, because it's tied to a larger belief system that is usually supported in your household. For me, my cultural background and religion were tied together because the church was a way for the first-generation immigrants within the community to come together and maintain a sense of who they were. So for me, religion had a compounding effect because it was directly paired with my culture.

A significant cultural element I mentioned earlier is the concept of the Evil Eye. This is linked to the way people see you enjoying your money. What's really interesting to me about the Egyptian culture that I was exposed to is the conflicting messaging between earning a good living and enjoying money. From my perspective, I see the emphasis on the importance of a good, well-paying career with all the prestige that comes with earning money. There's also not-so-subtle messaging around not wanting people to see that you had money because you don't want to attract the Evil Eye, or appear to be bragging. As a result, I'd see huge limitations placed on the way money was enjoyed.

An example like this can be an impactful one because we can see how the layering effect of messaging has an additional influence. When we aren't aware of it, we don't fully understand the impact. But when we gift ourselves the perspective of conscious understanding of the layers of our influences, we uplift ourselves with the power of choice. When we see what we can choose from, then we can truly make informed decisions that work best for us.

Chapter 9

Society

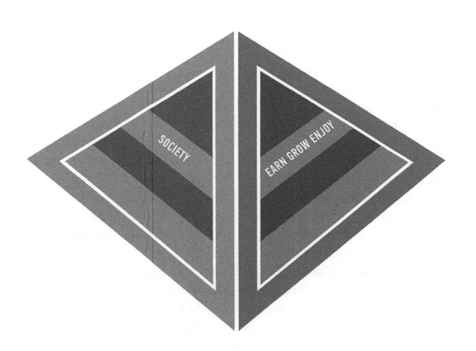

It is after becoming mature that any teaching succeeds.

—Egyptian Proverb

The next step in your storyline is emerging into adulthood, leaving your family's household and exploring the world outside of the community where you grew up. It's now time to situate yourself in the outside world. Many people believe that their emotions around money are only rooted in their upbringing, but there's so much more to it than that. Your origins, upbringing, and community essentially create the foundation of your money story, but now it's time to look at how that foundation has affected the way you see yourself fitting into society.

Society is a very broad term, encompassing a wide range of concepts, but what we're really talking about here are the rules and systems that unite us. These systems are a framework to navigate living and working with the people around us and in the world at large.

Up until this point of your life story, we've only been talking about the people that have had a direct and obvious influence on your feelings around money—your family, your teachers, your spiritual leaders, and so on. Now we're going to open up this discussion to look at how society has affected your financial situation. It's very easy to blame a certain system for why you're not earning, growing, or enjoying your money, but that's placing too much power on external forces. The awareness must come from inside you, and that's where change will occur.

An example of a system in our society that has a significant impact on one's limiting beliefs is the class system. Here in North America, we have a three-class system: upper class, middle class, and lower class. These definitions are based on one's socioeconomic position—or to put it very simply, how much money someone has. There's obviously more to it than that, but that's for the politicians and sociologists to debate. For our discussion, we're going to go with this very simplified definition. Your economic position within society can be particularly powerful in determining how you feel about money. Where you believe you fit into society can create a distance from a true sense of yourself because you have internalized what's being told to you about that position. This is a limiting belief and affects your Earn-Grow-Enjoy Model, which can be seen in some of the most mundane interactions.

I was flying to California, connecting through Chicago. My flight into Chicago was delayed, and I was rushing to get to the gate for my connection. As I approached the gate where the boarding line had formed, I politely asked someone in line if they knew what zone number was being loaded. I remember her face as she looked to her husband, then back to me and said, "Don't worry. We're in the last zone because we're poor." My heart broke as I heard the erroneous implications of that thought. My instinct was to correct the woman—the airline was simply boarding the plane to maximize efficiency, not based on ticket prices. For her, it wasn't about the facts. It was about the feelings and the beliefs around the segregation of classes. She believed that she belonged to the lower class; therefore, she was destined to board the plane last. There was so much hurt and negativity behind this woman's response. And even though we'd only met briefly, I still think about that interaction today.

Afterward, I remember reflecting on just how much we internalize societal messaging and the differentiation of the classes in a way that ends up limiting us. In that woman's statement, she demonstrated a limiting belief that she was poor. Statements like these are more powerful than we give them credit for. No matter what the motivation was behind her comment, it was a reflection of internal emotions resulting from a layering of life experiences and influences.

This type of limiting belief also applies to the other systems we're going to address in the next few chapters, including higher education, the media, the tax system, and the financial industry. These are all areas that are regulated by society and have a direct influence on our individual perspective on money. The suggestions coming from these areas can so easily become hidden within ourselves because the messages go unnoticed.

Especially when you're talking about something as huge as the society you live in, you can fall into the trap of saying, "This is just the way it is" or "It's normal." These thoughts imply that you've accepted and internalized your place in the world without question.

The impact of this acceptance is that you may feel defeated. Making changes in your life to improve your financial situation seems pointless, because how are you going to fight a whole system that's working against you? But as you build understanding and awareness, you'll begin to see the ideas you wish to let in and those that are simply holding you back.

Chapter 10

How Society Affects
Earning Money

Do not say "I am learned"; betake yourself to become wise.

—Egyptian Proverb

Earning money really is based in the systems of society, more so than anything else presented so far. Yes, the way you earn money is rooted in your origins, upbringing, and community; however, those were more historical influences. Now we're talking about how you've internalized those influences and applied them to your current situation. In this chapter, we're going to explore three specific areas that affect your perspective on earning money in society, including higher education, the media, and government tax systems. Whether you realize it or not, these systems are currently playing a role in your *perception* of earning money, as well as how you're *actually* earning it. These are large and very complex systems, but by bringing awareness to your perception of each one, we're going to shift your view toward the positive.

HIGHER EDUCATION

Our current society really does glorify higher education. There's a societal perception that we should be accumulating information through education; and then we rely on our degrees, diplomas, and certifications to define our earning potential. But within this thought process, the ideas around building knowledge through self-development and awareness are missing. We're looking to classrooms, textbooks, and lecture halls to define us, without a desire to define ourselves. But there's more to defining our earning potential than just getting pieces of paper. A positive relationship with earning money comes from within ourselves.

In my experiences and observations of the education system, both as a student and a teacher, I've found that we're taught from the outside in versus the inside out. Many people use education as a way to tell them who they are; this is an example of approaching it from the outside in. But if we start from a place of knowing ourselves, then we can use education to develop skills that enhance who we are; this is approaching knowledge from the inside out. Famed businessman Warren Buffett captured this sentiment perfectly when he said, "The best investment you can make, is an investment in yourself. …The more you learn, the more you'll earn."

Contrary to what society has told us, though, the connection between earning a degree and earning money is more complex than you might think. This idea is reflected in the Law of Compensation as outlined by Bob Proctor of the Proctor Gallagher Institute. This idea states that the amount of money you earn is a reflection of the need for your services, your ability to do a certain job, and how difficult it is to replace you. This is a complex topic, so I'm barely scratching the surface as I introduce it here. However, it's important to understand as you start to shift your thinking away from external factors and start to look from within.

The Law of Compensation and your beliefs about how money is earned provide a great place to start building your understanding of this concept. At this point, I encourage you to think about why you chose to study what you did and why you took your particular career path. Education can certainly be a stepping-stone to help you move forward; however, don't let yourself get caught up in the idea that education is going to give you a place in the world.

I'm presenting information about the Law of Compensation because it's a great example of seeing you at the center of it all. It's only in becoming your true self that you can earn more in the way that you want. And that doesn't necessarily mean through higher education. I want to be clear that I love education, so much so that I earned a degree in it, and it became the foundation on which I built my financial practice. A strong belief of mine has always been that education should be something that helps amplify you versus defining you. Education needs to work for who you are. When you start from a place of knowing yourself, then higher education serves to uplift you. But when you enter into higher education with feelings of obligation or uncertainty, then you're not going to get the results you desire—that is, a meaningful career path with unlimited earning potential.

THE MEDIA

When it comes to societal views and beliefs, the media can provide an excellent reflection of our world. The famed Canadian philosopher and media theorist Marshall McLuhan summed it up nicely when he said,

"Historians and archaeologists will one day discover that the ads of our time are the richest and most faithful reflections that any society ever made of its entire range of activities." Essentially, media is a true snapshot of exactly what's going on in society at any given time. Most of us enjoy consuming media (TV shows, movies, books, online content, and so on) that we connect with. And those who are producing media are always looking to tap into what society is talking about in the moment. This is where the reflection comes in. Media is simply reflecting back to us what we already are.

With money, the common theme I've observed is negativity. Money is just so easy to hate and is regularly demonized, or seen as the "bad guy." In the need to find something or someone to blame for all the world's problems, money is a bull's-eye. It's something that I grew up with, but didn't fully understand until I was an adult, and more specifically as a parent. I remember watching a kid's show with my son and seeing one family that was portrayed differently. Everyone in the cartoon community was getting along, being helpful, and working as a team, except this one family. The family was rude, demeaning, and boastful. What was fundamentally different about this family? Money. They were the only ones who were materially wealthy. The link became clear through the messaging that money was the root of their unseemly behavior toward everyone else in the community. In my discomfort, I took this teachable moment to have a discussion with my son about attitudes and choices. The root of my messaging was the fact that money can't choose anything—only we can make decisions, and that particular family was choosing their own behavior. It wasn't being dictated to them by the money they had.

This moment with my son made my mind wander through my own memories and experiences with the media. How many times had I seen money being portrayed as the cause of a problem? Or as the villain? It's these subtle but repetitive messages that we absorb over and over again that we internalize without really understanding where they came from. No one questions when the rich guy at the end of the movie is the villain—in fact, that storyline has become so repetitive that it's a cliché. Don't get me wrong, I'm not demonizing the media, but like everything else, there are positives and negatives. If we don't acknowledge and build an awareness of the negative, we won't be able to see, focus, and shift toward the positive.

There's a powerful and popular belief, which still exists today, that says that having money or earning more money is the cause of problems, worries, and stresses. Pop culture icon The Notorious B.I.G. summed up this idea nicely when he rapped, "Mo Money Mo Problems" in the 1997 megahit. This is still a commonly used reference more than 20 years later because it really captures a widespread belief. The idea that more money has a direct correlation with more problems is a powerful one because of just how limiting it is. If you believe this idea, then you may easily make decisions that will lead you to earn less money, even if you aren't aware of it. You could avoid asking for a promotion, or choose not to pursue a career development opportunity. Money then becomes tied in with fear, because you're afraid of opening yourself up to negative consequences or "mo problems." But what we really need to realize is that everyone has problems, worry, and stress no matter what their income is—the difference is in what we choose to focus on.

The media is a powerful influence because of the passive attitude we take with it and the way we can easily internalize ideas at face value without critical thinking. Consuming media can also reinforce messaging you've received at other layers of your Pyramid of Financial Influences. When you hear the same message over and over again, you can believe it without questioning it, and it becomes a limiting belief. The media is a perfect example of this internalization through repetition. Simply by putting a little thought into the information you're receiving (or recognize), you will become empowered to evaluate (or reconcile) whether or not the message is uplifting or limiting. If it's limiting, it's time to let it go (or release). And then repeat this process.

THE TAX SYSTEM

Our tax system can very easily lead to one of the most negative conversations around money. It's one we all love to hate, and a part of the reason for that is that it's something we don't want and can't control. In every layer of our Pyramid of Financial Influences, we have been conditioned, and even encouraged, to despise taxes. I'd go so far as to say that complaining about taxes is a socially acceptable conversation, and people would probably look at you strangely if you went against that norm.

What this conditioning has done is to direct our focus and energy completely toward the negative, and it becomes just another one of our limiting factors. When we direct our focus toward something that is not in our control, we leave the door wide open for negativity. As we've already discussed, when something is negative, we tend to avoid it as much as possible. Why would we want to deal with something that brings up feelings of stress, worry, or sadness? What ends up happening is that we only focus on what we don't want through a lens of our negative feelings and avoidance.

When we focus on what we don't want, that's all we're going to get. I often connect this idea with the imagery of a pothole in the road. Picture yourself driving a car and you see a pothole on the road ahead of you that you definitely want to avoid. As you're driving toward it, you can't help but look at the pothole and say to yourself, "I don't want to hit that pothole. I don't want to hit that pothole. I don't want to hit that pothole." When you get to the pothole, what do you think is going to happen? All you're going to do is get exactly what you didn't want—you're going to hit the pothole. When we direct our gaze and our thoughts toward what we don't want, that's exactly what we end up getting because what's holding our attention will dictate our direction and results.

Instead, let's reverse that perspective and start focusing on what you do want. If you want to earn more money, then that's where your focus should be. With this mind-set, your entire perspective on taxation can change to the positive. Taxes are inevitable. There's no escaping that fact. The key to turning this concept into a positive is to focus on yourself at the center of your thinking, and think about the aspects that you can control. One of the biggest limiting beliefs that I've consistently heard in my practice as a financial planner is the idea of avoiding earning more money for fear of paying more taxes. But that's approaching the situation from a negative perspective, and focusing on what you don't want—that is, paying more taxes. But when you remove this limiting belief, you're opening yourself up for more earning potential.

Let's talk some real numbers now through a very simplistic example. As you start earning additional income, you're also paying additional taxes. Let's assume a high tax rate of 50 percent. That means that for every $10,000 you earn, you will also pay $5,000 in taxes. The key difference is in the way you feel and think about these numbers. Rather than saying, "I'm paying $5,000 in taxes," why not shift your mind-set to, "I'm earning an extra $5,000!" If all you focused on was the tax increase, you may have avoided building your income and wouldn't have an extra $5,000 in your pocket. And the best part about earning more money is that it doesn't have to stop there. In this example, I am assuming no tax planning or preparation. But as you earn more, you can equip yourself with the tools, resources, and access to professionals that will help you increase your wealth even further. As you start to focus on what you want, you'll also be taking a proactive approach to your money… and get out of the cycle of avoidance.

Chapter 11

How Society Affects
Growing Money

Do not do a thing that you have not first examined.

—Egyptian Proverb

Now that we've looked at how three of society's systems can affect your feelings around earning money, let's shift the focus to a system that helps you grow your money: the financial sector, which encompasses many different industries, including the banking system, stock markets, insurance, investments, real estate, and much more. The financial sector is not only regulated by society, it really is at the heart of our society's economy. Without financial industries, we wouldn't have an economic structure. This topic is particularly close to my heart, and one of the driving forces of my life's work is to change the conversation around finances. And changing the conversation also means changing one's connection with the financial industry.

This is the largest system that we look at to provide us with the opportunities to grow our money. Whether we're opening a bank account or building an investment portfolio, the financial industry is where we must turn. Many of us have strong feelings and firsthand experiences with this industry that need to be reconciled before we can utilize this system to service our individual financial goals.

You see, when we're looking to break the negative Make-Spend Cycle with the idea of saving, it's the financial industry that we turn to. We've seen that the individual elements of the Make-Spend Cycle, which includes attempts to insert "save" somewhere in the process, are all based on negative feelings; and whether we recognize it or not, we try to insert a positive to change things. There's a popular term that we turn to in the financial industry to try and encourage change: *financial empowerment*. From afar, the term seems positive and well-meaning, even empowering. But even when we try to implement this idea, we either still end up with the same negative results or the change doesn't last long. Why is that? The answer is in our feelings and our beliefs around what financial empowerment is.

At this point in the conversation, we know that our feelings and beliefs around money didn't just appear; rather, they were formed over time. We've reviewed the individual layers in our Pyramid of Financial Influences and discovered that when it comes to growing or managing our money, we really didn't have any hands-on exposure until we reach this point in our money story. This leaves us unsure of ourselves, because it's something we don't fully understand. And as a result, we turn to the financial industry with the belief that the professionals know better, leaving us ultimately feeling powerless.

That belief comes through a depreciating feeling of ourselves in our understanding and ability to manage the way we grow our money, culminating in a lack of confidence with managing our money. That lack of confidence is a significant contributor to avoidance. Essentially, the financial industry is something we don't understand, we're disconnected from it, and quite frankly, we don't want to deal with it. You see, when we don't understand something within us, we go looking for the solution outside of us, and by applying that strategy, we don't get the results we want. What I present to you here is that the solutions reside within each of us individually.

While we're speaking about ourselves as individuals here, keep in mind that we're also discussing societal structures and popular beliefs. Many of us have a certain belief and idea of what financial empowerment is because most of us didn't have the exposure to managing our money in order to form a personalized understanding of it. This happens with people in every walk of life and at every income bracket because just about everyone went through those first layers of their own pyramid. I say this because with lower confidence, we feel that we're the only ones that feel this way, and everyone else seems to have it all together. That simply isn't true. At the same time, just because so many feel this way doesn't mean we can't effect positive change.

We're having these conversations because I firmly believe we can. I've seen the positive shift take place more times than I can tell you, and the beauty of it never gets old. This is what I want for you—to have true and meaningful financial empowerment.

FINANCIAL EMPOWERMENT FROM THE OUTSIDE IN

To create different results related to financial empowerment, let's first get a clear image of what we've been trying to implement repeatedly in an effort to achieve different results. To try gaining or building confidence with our finances, we naturally turn to the financial industry for empowerment, because when we don't understand something, we turn to those who do. But the way we do so is what makes all the difference. When we approach this concept with low confidence and negative feelings, we're met with ideas, strategies, structures, and a plethora of information that all seems to be communicated to us in acronyms and jargon.

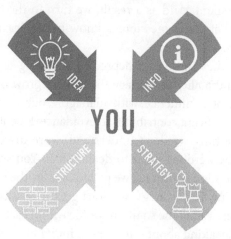

Then, we adhere to the popular belief that financial empowerment means memorizing, internalizing, and trying to fit into different financial ideas, strategies, and so on. We started from a negative place and not having confidence in ourselves, so we approach financial empowerment based on someone else's definition of what it means. True financial empowerment, however, can only be defined by *you* because it only applies to *you*. Financial Em*power*ment emanates from within. It comes from understanding yourself as you relate to money.

True financial empowerment comes from connecting to your inner power through understanding your formed feelings and beliefs about money and then actively shifting to the positive with your choices. That is exactly what we're doing here together. Through your true financial empowerment, the entire direction of everything changes as it becomes directed outward from you.

FINANCIAL EMPOWERMENT FROM THE INSIDE OUT

The key to forming a connection with financial industries and creating a positive shift in your life is to regain power over your own results. We often look at financial industries as something different and separate from everything else in our lives. This makes sense, because many people view money as something separate from themselves as well.

We fail to recognize that who we are as individuals is directly connected to our financial situation. In reality, our finances are a part of our day-to-day lives, so much so that it's the fuel that helps us move forward. If we're stuck in a pattern of believing that we are separate from our money, then we're going to be weighed down by the negative. To break the cycle, we must start connecting to our internal power and shifting our thought patterns to the positive.

You are the essential starting place; and every financial tool, strategy, or idea is incidental because it's meant to serve you, rather than you serving it. Every financial idea, product, or structure revolves around you and your direction. You're not meant to fit into a template or formula created by the financial industry. So when you understand yourself, you begin to look for something very different from that industry. A meaningful shift in perspective takes place as you no longer look to financial professionals as *experts*—but instead as *specialists*. This may seem like a small change, but I assure you it's far from small.

There's a significant difference between the feeling and belief behind the words *expert* versus *specialist*, and our own personal confidence is at the center of that difference. When you say the word expert, it often comes from a place of low self-confidence, where you're putting someone (in this case, a financial professional) above you. When you look at the idea of a specialist, however, the belief behind that word is very different. This term represents a team approach in which you appreciate and know yourself and what you wish to accomplish.

Changing that perspective is how the financial industry serves you, rather than you having the feeling that you're serving it. As such, you build confidence and an understanding of yourself and what you want for yourself. Now the information becomes centered and directed from the inside out— as it always should, because with this idea, *you* are the subject-matter expert.

This may sound like a foreign concept because it's different from what we're used to. To help make sense of it, let's use an example that we can better relate to and connect with: going to see a medical professional. Whether you're going to see a general practitioner, naturopath, or anything in between, you're the advocate for your own health and wellness. When you sit down with this individual, he or she is the specialist in the respective practice, and you are the specialist in *you*. The medical professional is there to serve you and help you achieve your health and wellness goals.

The only way health professionals can add value or benefit you is when you're able to tell them exactly how you feel and what you want. Everything that they're going to recommend is based on your knowledge and connection with yourself. The concept of financial empowerment that I explained to you is no different from that. When you see your health professional, you are the central figure, and everything is directed from you, which is exactly the way it should be with the financial industry.

This conversation is near and dear to my heart for so many reasons, starting with the fact that it's the industry I became a part of in order to make a difference and create positive change, one client at a time. I built my practice on the foundation of education, understanding, and helping my clients develop a positive connection with themselves and their finances. What I recognized is that in order to want to grow your money, you must see value and importance in it. To see that value and importance, you must have a positive connection to the value of yourself, your goals, and your desires. With this thought on its own, there is a balance. When you have a positive connection and understanding of yourself and your needs, you surround yourself with the right team who will speak your language.

What we're doing here is significant because it's not what we've been taught about the starting place of managing our money. We've been taught to put together a task list and try to inject savings somewhere in the Make-Spend Cycle. Sometimes, it's through budgeting with the good intention of setting money aside between making money and spending it. Others make money, spend money (that is, pay bills), and then hope there's some money left over to save. Even saying the idea of making a task or to-do list doesn't sound enticing. The reason is simple—it isn't an enticing proposition because it's based on everything and everyone else. But in either situation, people are taking a passive approach, which is a direct reflection on their lack of connection to the process.

The way you actually break the negative Make-Spend Cycle is to shift your thought process to the Earn-Grow-Enjoy Model, with you at the center. In this model, you become far more connected to yourself and what you actually want. Closing down those outside influences and turning inward is the only way to break the cycle of negativity around your finances. So, let's shift that cycle to the positive in the most meaningful way, through a connection with yourself. Growing your money allows you to do more of what you want to do and achieve, and it magnifies your goals. With this in mind, the importance of having a positive relationship with money becomes even more important.

Chapter 12

How Society Affects Enjoying Money

Yesterday's drunkenness does not quench today's thirst.

—Egyptian Proverb

When it comes to the influence of society, one of the most important things that I see as a financial professional is the expectation around enjoying our money. We touched on the idea of class separation in a previous chapter, but I'd like to come back to the concept of class as we discuss how to enjoy our money. As we've already established, in North America, we have a three-class system: upper, middle, and lower. And for the sake of simplicity, we're looking at the separation of class based only on how much money someone has. People's self-worth can be so intertwined with their perceived class status that decisions are made only based around where they think they belong in society. This perceived status then becomes a huge limiting belief.

So often we internalize messages that come from outside of ourselves, especially when making decisions about what to buy or not buy. The idea of enjoying money can be more emotionally charged than the Earn-Grow portion of our model because it can be seen by others, in the way we discussed enjoying money in the context of community comparison. It's under these watchful eyes that you can feel an immense pressure to fit in with your surrounding society, specifically within the class you perceive yourself to be a part of.

In this case, enjoying money can come from a place of appearance and expectation, rather than from your own internal definition of enjoyment. And these expectations can manifest in negative ways. Some people may look for outward expressions of wealth, or the "keeping up the Joneses" mentality, while others will feel the need to hide their wealth so they don't alienate those around them. In either situation, decisions around enjoying money are being influenced by the need to fit into the class that you think you belong to. But where's your definition of enjoyment? What is it that *you* enjoy? These are the answers you need to be focusing on—with you at the center.

Think back. Were there ever purchases you made because you felt a sense of obligation, guilt, or pressure? Many of us have, including myself. Where I was growing up, I believed that owning a specific type of luxury vehicle was an indication of success. Once someone made that type of purchase, it was a way to communicate to those around you that you'd "made it" and were a part of a certain class. It seemed to me that it didn't even matter if the person actually liked the car—it was all about what that car represented: status and success.

Enjoying money comes from a connection to our own concepts of happiness. People who buy these types of cars as status symbols may never have any feelings of joy about it. They're just objects that were accumulated for reasons influenced by society. These individuals simply internalized the idea that the car would make them happy, without stopping to consider whether or not that's actually true for them.

I certainly felt this societal pressure, especially as I was searching for my own sense of belonging. As I previously mentioned, I grew up in a humble home in a wealthy community. Because of this situation, I wasn't considered to be in the same societal class as those around me. If I had internalized this assumption, then I could have very easily taken a different view of spending my own money today—that is, I would probably just be spending it, not enjoying it.

When speaking about the topic of enjoying money, out of pure curiosity, people often ask me how I do so. That's an easy answer for me. I've always loved cars. From the time I was a young girl, there's nothing that brought me greater joy than being in a car (or talking about cars or reading about cars). I also had a special crush on a particular car for as long as I can remember. It wasn't the most popular car, and it certainly didn't scream, "You've made it!" the way that some other cars did. But none of that mattered. Just the thought of this car, even today, brings a joyful smile to my face. And I knew that one day I would own that car. For me, it was something I wanted to earn, and the hard work it took for me to buy it would only add to the enjoyment once I reached my goal. This was something for me. My desire for this car came from no one else but me.

As I grew up and I told the people around me about my goal, the consistent messaging that I heard was that I was going to have to marry someone who could buy me my dream car. Because of the foundational layers of my upbringing and the reinforced messaging I got from my community, and as an adult, society also told me that the only way I would reach my goal was to marry someone above my class. That was a message I refused to internalize. Instead, I used it as fuel for my fire. It became a fact that I was going to buy that car with my own earnings when the time was right to make such a major purchase. And I did. With a grateful and joyous heart, I bought my dream car. Because of the meaning behind my purchase, I enjoy every bit of that car—especially my internal (and sometimes external) giddy giggle when I hear the engine rev as I accelerate to merge onto the highway. Do you think I would have the same smile on my face if I'd settled for something because it was better suited to my "class"? Or if I had aspired to purchase a different car as a way to prove that I'd "made it"?

So, I ask you now, what is *your* motivation in your purchasing decisions? Is it internal or external to you? When your decision comes internally, you'll find true and meaningful enjoyment that is defined only by you. So, start with the right motivation, build a meaningful goal, and then follow through with a success-oriented mind-set. If you do so, you'll find that you will appreciate and enjoy the purchases you make, and that feeling will come from a positive and meaningful place.

Chapter 13

Relationships

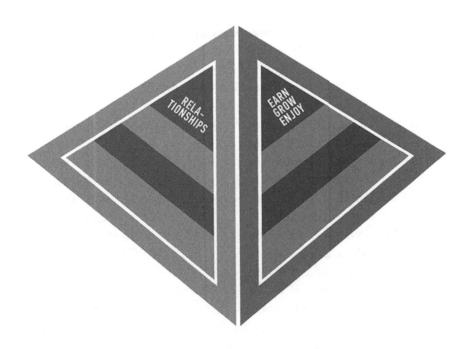

If I knew you and you knew me,
If both of us could clearly see,
And with an inner sight divine,
The meaning of your heart and mine,
I'm sure that we would differ less,
And clasp our hands in friendliness;
Our thoughts would pleasantly agree,
If I knew you and you knew me.

—Nixon Waterman

Of all the layers of influence that we've talked about so far, relationships really serve to highlight just how complex our feelings around money can be. Money plays a role in all relationships—not just romantic ones—but also those with your family members, friends, colleagues, and even casual acquaintances. At some point in any relationship, money is going to be involved, even if it's as simple as who's buying coffee or how to split the dinner bill. But for our discussion here, we're going to focus on marriages and committed romantic relationships.

One of the greatest assets—and challenges—for couples is communication. Famed author and life coach Tony Robbins really captured this sentiment when he said, "The way we communicate with others and with ourselves ultimately determines the quality of our lives." When it comes to money, the lines of communication often break down. The language we use is muddied with assumptions to fill in the blanks left from a lack of clear communication and understanding.

Money problems are consistently listed as one of the main reasons why couples get divorced. In fact, the Institute for Divorce Financial Analysts cites that "money issues" account for 22 percent of divorces in the U.S.. Common conflicts that arise include debt management, spending habits, hiding money from each other, and using money as a form of control. While these conflicts are important to explore, in my experience working with couples, what's actually at the root of these issues stems from the Pyramid of Financial Influences.

You see, if you don't have a clear understanding of your own financial baggage, how can you effectively work through these issues with someone else? Your money story has led to expectations, and your partner comes to the relationship with an entirely separate money story and resulting expectations. People need to first understand themselves *before* they can come together effectively. The process of unraveling your financial influences is really what's lacking in so many premarital preparations (whether it's formal preparation such as a course or counseling, or a couple simply having tough conversations on their own).

I started this chapter with a beautiful poem by Nixon Waterman. I love this poem for many reasons, but in particular, it's because the poem serves as a reminder that when we know and understand ourselves, we better understand someone else. Up until this point, your layers of influence have run parallel with those of the other person. Your storylines start to intersect at this point in the pyramid. If you haven't done the work to understand your other layers (Origins and Upbringing, Community and Society), you won't be able to see yourself; and as a result, the lines of communication blur with unclear thoughts and assumptions.

There is just so much that isn't directly communicated in words. Sometimes, it's what isn't said that makes a greater impact. Some of the things that so often go unsaid are the assumptions we make inside our own heads and then imprint onto someone else. Researcher Brené Brown has talked extensively about the phrase "the story I'm making up is..." During her Netflix special *The Call to Courage*, she recounts an incident that happened while she was swimming with her husband, where she was trying to get his attention but he wasn't responding. The "story she was making up" was that he wasn't acknowledging her because he was lost in his thoughts about how old she was, or that she no longer looked good in a bathing suit, or that she was a bad swimmer. This assumption caused her to feel ashamed and embarrassed, and it ultimately led to conflict with her husband. But in reality, the reason her husband wasn't responding to her was that he was having a panic attack. It was the assumption that led to the conflict. The reality of the situation was quite different.

In my practice, when I'm working with couples, I've personally witnessed this type of conflict. But in most cases, the assumption was actually a battle that was occurring internally, and it was being projected onto the other person. In Brown's example, she was already feeling insecure and projected that narrative onto her husband. When we haven't reconciled our own internal battles, we mirror it onto the other person in the relationship.

Up until this point in your life, chances are that you haven't had the opportunity to develop a comprehensive understanding of your belief system around money. In addition, you haven't been taught to speak about it because throughout the layers of your Pyramid of Financial Influences, money was observed but not spoken about, leaving the conversation to indirectly develop internally. It's through this layering that you've formed feelings, expectations, and beliefs throughout your life that haven't been fully recognized, reconciled, or released. But if you can't explain your own feelings around money, how can you expect to explain them to the person you're in a relationship with? This is the heart of so many conflicts—you just haven't been given the vocabulary to even have the conversation. When you see, understand, and have an awareness of your own perspective, it's much easier to see things from the other person's perspective as well. When you know yourself and are deeply connected to who you are, it is then that you and your partner can create a meaningful connection on a level playing field.

In our conversation so far, we've gained perspective and understanding on the influences of our origins, upbringing, community, and society. Within each of these pyramid layers, we've encountered numerous experiences and influences, each having their own perspectives and intricacies. Those perspectives and details are the stones of the pyramid—the building blocks—so to speak. However, without having the opportunity to connect to our experiences, we enter into a relationship with a limited, one-dimensional view of ourselves and money. Even in preparing for a committed relationship by having what is often referred to as the "dreaded money conversation," the most common question that's asked is, "What are your expectations?" I consistently see this being a difficult question for most—and understandably so. How can we accurately answer this question if we don't know what our expectations really are or how they came to be? The result is often forced responses that are unclear and aren't truly accurate.

This disconnect can result in feeling like each person in the relationship is speaking a different language. And in a way, each one really is. Without having a full understanding of yourself and your own perspectives around money, you can't explain the money language that you speak, nor can you translate the language of your partner. The result is that you can't communicate your expectations because you don't fully understand them yourself. And this fundamental misunderstanding starts to manifest in your relationship in various ways, some I've already mentioned: conflict around debt management and spending habits, hiding money, and using money as a control tactic.

Without fully understanding yourself, a natural reaction is to avoid the conversation altogether, because it brings up feelings that are unpleasant and confrontational. This discomfort and lack of connection can make you feel like things are out of control, and you react instead of respond, which only fuels the negative cycle. Bob Proctor put it beautifully: "When you react you are giving away power. When you respond you are staying in control of yourself." That reaction is what I've consistently witnessed firsthand as a cause of confrontation, anger, disappointment, and hurt. These are not positive feelings, so people jump to the reaction of avoidance.

On the other side of this reaction is the idea of response. The difference between the two comes from everything that we've discussed so far: perspective, understanding, and conscious awareness leading to positive choice. As you continue to work through these concepts, you'll find that something very powerful changes—your approach. The reaction of *confrontation* transforms into the response of *communication*. The difference is a conversation as opposed to a battle. The approach of a conversation is to communicate how you're feeling and what you're thinking about with a heartfelt desire to understand the perspective, feelings, and thoughts of your partner. Then, your partner has is be willing to do the same.

This skill is one I encourage everyone I work with to develop, and one that I apply in my own life. When applied effectively, there is a significant shift to the positive. This is why this conversation is one that I'm particularly passionate about. I've seen and experienced how central it is to so many of our lives, and relationships are no exception. A shift from confrontation to communication means a change from negative assumptions to positive understanding. With confrontation, we grow apart; with communication, we grow together. Here, we're developing the tools to grow together, starting by approaching yourself in a positive light.

As you begin to think about your Earn-Grow-Enjoy Model in the context of your relationship, consider the expectations and assumptions you make, and where in your Pyramid of Financial Influences, those came from. In addition, give some thought to your other relationships (platonic and romantic), and the influence they have on your current (or future) relationships. If money is at the center of so many unpleasant conversations in a relationship, chances are it was there in past relationships, and may even have been the reason for dissolving those relationships. With those experiences and resulting feelings being unresolved, we bring that with us to the next relationship by often unintentionally imprinting them on our new partner. Here, we have the opportunity to *recognize*, *reconcile*, and *release* what doesn't serve or uplift us.

Conscious awareness also brings about a positive focus. When you've let go of what you don't want, you can focus on what you *do* want, shifting from the negative to the positive. This is the freeing feeling that I want for you. Having a strong and positive money connection in your relationship propels you forward in your ability to earn, grow, and enjoy together.

THE RELATIONSHIP-MONEY COMMUNICATION CYCLE

So often, you might find that you're unhappy with the conversation about money, and it results in conflict. You're unhappy, but you can't fully explain why. As you begin to understand the perspective of your views and beliefs around money, you can then apply that knowledge to effective and meaningful conversations in your relationship. When you each come to the table with an understanding of yourselves first, then you can have meaningful conversations together, rather than feeling like you're in different rooms.

The importance of applying a positive and effective communication cycle around money can't be overstated. Learning to implement this is a skill that will continue to benefit your relationship. You will each grow and develop as individuals, and then as a couple, creating richness in your communication.

The challenge that we're working to overcome as individuals is that we haven't learned to have our own financial discussions within ourselves, so it makes sense that we haven't been able to participate in a productive one with our partners. We're now building on the awareness that we've been developing from the previous layers of the pyramid.

At this point, you're honing skills to do what once seemed impossible—making the financial discussion approachable, positive, and enjoyable. Yes, I said enjoyable. The key here is that you've started this process from the most effective place—within you. Having a healthy, clear, and open line of communication around money relieves a significant burden on your relationship, and it makes room for each of you to become more of yourselves as individuals.

Having an understanding of the negative communication cycle allows for an appreciation of the positive cycle. All we need to do from here is to become aware of what's taking place, and choose the style of communication cycle we want to implement. Without an understanding of what's happening, we're often playing the negative cycle on repeat, having no idea why things aren't getting better. To effect positive change, we need to first understand what it is we want to change, and that starts from within. To better understand communication cycles, let's look at a visual of both the negative and positive models.

THE NEGATIVE RELATIONSHIP-MONEY COMMUNICATION CYCLE

Uncommunicated Expectations: This issue often stems from a lack of understanding of yourself and your money story. You may perceive something as "normal" through the lens of your experiences and associated beliefs. And because you believe it's normal, you may feel that communication about it isn't necessary because it's so obvious. Whether you understand your background or not, if you don't communicate your beliefs, your partner won't understand where you're coming from.

Assumptions: With a lack of information, humans are predisposed to making snap decisions. Your brain is trained to filling in the blanks, and this likely occurs as the result of erroneous information, and where uncommunicated expectations are applied.

Misunderstanding: The concept of moving forward on something with wrong information.

Conflict: Verbal or nonverbal negative reactions. These can happen in many ways, from the minor and mundane to a big blowup. In a reaction, we lose control of ourselves, and we're riding a roller coaster of emotions that we feel we have no power over.

Avoidance: Because conflict is negative, we avoid it, and we restart the negative cycle again.

THE POSITIVE RELATIONSHIP-MONEY COMMUNICATION CYCLE

Self-Awareness: Understanding your pyramid layers gives you knowledge of where your views and beliefs came from. Therefore, you gain an appreciation for the way you see things and why.

Clear and Open Communication: With your self-awareness, each person is able to do what wasn't possible before—clearly communicate the way you see things and why. You can now explain your beliefs and see where they came from.

Perspective: This is when you gain an understanding of your partner's personal journey, and your partner understands yours.

Meaningful Connection: Here, you're able to respond. Instead of riding the roller coaster, you're observing it and communicating from a higher level. In addition, instead of feeling disconnected, you're now connected to each other and on the same page.

Keep Going!: Although this sounds rosy, it doesn't mean that there aren't disagreements. This style allows for more constructive discussions that are response oriented, instead of reactionary. Relationships are dynamic, not static, because you each keep growing … and so must the relationship.

THE LOVE STORY OF JOE AND JANE

To better understand these cycles, let's look at a lighthearted example outside of money based on a couple who had just moved in together. In this story, the couple each had their own place before getting married. For simplicity's sake, let's call them Joe and Jane.

This is a love story that starts with genuine devotion and admiration. Joe wanted to be thoughtful and caring toward Jane, who was incredibly tidy. Before they moved in together, he had decided that he would do what he could to contribute to the cleanliness of the house. He didn't vocalize it because he learned growing up that, if you were going to be helpful, you didn't need to be boastful by saying anything about it. You should just do it because it's the right thing to do.

Every morning after they each showered, Joe noticed Jane's habit of haphazardly draping the wet towels over the towel bar, rather than folding them neatly. Because of his love and devotion for his wife, he thought he would help with this task. So, every morning after Jane showered, he would fold the towels in the bathroom with a feeling that he was contributing in keeping the house tidy.

Feeling proud of his contribution, Joe would head to the kitchen for breakfast. But as he passed the bathroom on his way out the door to work, he'd notice that the towels were unfolded once again and draped over the towel rack. With frustration this time, he'd fold the towels again and leave. For years in their marriage, this would be the regular morning routine, with neither of them saying a word to each other.

The lessons from Joe's upbringing around helping without being boastful were louder than his need to bring up this issue with his wife— that is, until one day, after breakfast, Jane went into the bathroom and let out a huge sigh as she stomped into the kitchen with a towel in her hand. His first thought was, *What could possibly have her so upset? I just folded those so neatly.* With years of bottled up anger behind her, she yelled, "Ever since we got married, I've been cleaning up after you! I spread out the wet towels to dry nicely, and you keep folding them and making them musty! Stop it!" Feeling hurt by what Joe felt like a lack of appreciation for his efforts, he reacted by yelling back.

Even though things seemed fine on the surface, there was a negative cycle of communication lurking, and it started with uncommunicated expectations behind something that seemed so innocent to both of them. For Joe, his thought was to help his wife without saying anything; and for Jane, her thought was to let the damp towels dry so that they wouldn't get musty. For each of them, the idea seemed so basic, so "normal." With no communication to understand or clarify, they each assumed that saying something would either be boastful or offensive, so they chose to keep it to themselves. As a result, there was a misunderstanding over why the towels were folded and then unfolded. Over time, the frustration that was simmering got heated, and ultimately boiled over into a conflict. What they feared most and wanted to avoid is exactly what transpired in an intense manner. The same can be said for the financial communication cycle.

These cycles impact all aspects of our Earn-Grow-Enjoy Model in a relationship. In subsequent chapters, we'll review some examples of what those are. As you read them, be sure to think about the circumstances in your current relationship to gain a more comprehensive perspective of them. It's also beneficial to think about the different ways in which you talk (or don't talk) about money in your relationship.

Chapter 14

How Relationships Affect Earning Money

He who is gentle by virtue of his good character makes his own fate.

—Egyptian Proverb

If our uncommunicated expectations are a result of our experiences and influences, then they can be one of the most impactful things that we bring to a relationship, especially when it comes to our roles (or perceived roles) as partners or spouses. Taking into consideration all of the influences we've experienced until this point in our lives, at every layer there is messaging around the roles that individuals are expected to play. In many instances, we're specifically talking about gender roles, but there's more to it than that. These ingrained roles really do have a significant influence on how we feel we can earn money while in a relationship, and an equally significant influence on how we feel that our partners can earn money as well. The fact that the term breadwinner is still used to reflect the main income earner is evidence of that.

Let's consider our friends Joe and Jane again and offer some very brief context to their relationship. Joe's family has deep roots in America. His cultural background is mixed, and neither Joe nor his extended family has any real emotional connection outside of American culture. He grew up as an only child being raised by a hardworking single mom. She was very open-minded and involved in many social causes, valuing tolerance and acceptance above everything else. And these values were reinforced by Joe's surrounding community.

Jane comes from an immigrant family where gender roles are deeply rooted in her culture. She grew up watching her parents conform to very traditional roles in their relationship without question. The neighborhood in the small rural town she grew up in was densely populated with families of the same cultural background. As a teenager, she was very involved with the local church and cultural community center as well. It wasn't until she moved away from home to attend college in a major city that she began to consider her place in society outside of the gender and cultural roles she was assigned by her upbringing.

When they got married, Joe and Jane brought all these layers of influence with them to the relationship. They each knew about the other's upbringing, but, like most people, had never stopped to consider how those layers affect the expectations and assumptions they held for themselves and the other person. Early in their marriage, Jane defaulted to the role her mother exemplified as a wife, and Joe found that he liked being a part of a more traditional structure than he grew up with. Feeling the pressure to provide for his new family, Joe immediately accepted a high-paying position in a field he felt had great earning potential. Jane's priority was rooted in providing a comfortable home for her husband. She accepted a part-time administrative position but focused most of her energy on their new home. Their dynamic as a couple affected every aspect of their Earn-Grow-Enjoy Model.

Neither Joe nor Jane was connected to their Pyramid of Financial Influences in a meaningful way, which caused them to imprint their own expectations on the other person without realizing it. And just like with the towel example, there was a conflict in their set of beliefs, but they weren't able to pinpoint exactly what it was. This discomfort led to avoidance, which ultimately manifested in an explosive argument about a towel. Like so many situations in a relationship, viewpoints aren't one-dimensional. But at the heart of it, you need to understand yourself before you'll be able to communicate with and respond to someone else.

So what does this all have to do with earning money? Well, the way you earn money can be an expression of yourself through your skills, expertise, or passion. *Fulfillment* is often the term used to describe the feeling of living up to your potential. Feeling fulfilled with how you're earning money allows you to be more aligned with your true self. For this to be the case, a relationship must support your desire to become the best version of you. And often conflict arises when one partner wants to change the way in which he or she earns money. For many reasons, one partner may make the decision that the way their money is being earned needs to reflect his or her growing vision. The natural assumption, especially when factoring in this person's perceived role, is that the partner won't be supportive of the change. If the couple is caught in a negative communication cycle, then there's no way for them to have an open and productive conversation from a place of understanding.

This is where people start to feel stuck, and resentment toward the other person starts to build up. Let's be clear, though—at this point, no actual conversation has taken place, so feelings of resentment are based solely on an assumption that the partner won't be supportive. The way to initiate the conversation is to make that shift to a positive communication cycle—and this is exactly what I do with my clients. When I was leading a financial conversation, it would be less about the actual money, and more about effective communication. This directly reflected the positive financial results.

To better understand this cycle, let's walk through negative communication with Joe and Jane, from the perspective of Jane, who, after a few years into the marriage, was feeling unsatisfied with her administrative job and had a desire to expand her role. Several positions in the event planning division had opened up at her company in the last year, and based on her unique talents, Jane knew she'd be perfect for one of these roles. After some counseling, she was able to identify her passion and know that a career change of this type would lead to earning more money because it would allow her to be more of herself. With the uncommunicated expectations of the roles Joe and Jane had settled into, Jane's assumption was that Joe wouldn't be supportive of her career change, so she never told him about her desire. Because the lines of communication weren't open, Joe hadn't even been given the opportunity to discuss his feelings about the subject. The story Jane was telling herself in her head resulted in negative feelings and misunderstanding.

Even though Joe and Jane are fictional, I've seen situations like this over and over again, leading to conflict because one person has a desire (in this case, to change careers), and the other person is left feeling confused and isolated because he or she really doesn't know what's going on.

The conflict isn't pleasant, and ultimately leads to avoiding further conversations in an attempt to suppress the negative emotions tied to the issue. In my practice, I've helped facilitate conversations such as these many times. What I do each time is to demonstrate the negative communication cycle in order to shift it to the positive (essentially utilizing the 4R Process). We start with the individuals discussing their own self-awareness by explaining what they're thinking and where those thoughts are coming from. It sounds easy, but it's really not, especially if they haven't done the work to piece together where the belief system came from. With that newfound awareness, we're able to establish clear and open communication by gaining a perspective on the other person's viewpoints, hopefully with an added layer of empathy.

If you have a desire to earn more, you need to start with a belief in yourself, and not wait around for your partner to tell you that he or she believes in you. Solid relationships are built on a foundation of together but separate. You need to be truly connected to who you are and be willing to express yourself in a positive way in order for togetherness to work. In the case of Joe and Jane, Jane was so lost in her role of their togetherness that she wasn't even willing to talk to Joe about her desire to make a career change. Her anger and resentment just grew. Joe felt that something in their relationship had changed, but he had no way to express his confusion. What Jane didn't know—because she never asked—was that Joe was completely supportive of her changing careers, and in fact, he would have been relieved if she had done so.

You see, during Jane's self-exploration, Joe had come to his own realization that he was feeling immense pressure in his role because it was taking him away from who he really was. If Jane was able to increase her earnings, then Joe would be able to focus on the social causes he was so passionate about but had put aside when he assumed the traditional role of "breadwinner." Joe had the idea to approach his boss about taking over the company's charitable activities, allowing him to combine his executive experience with his social advocacy work. But he had devalued himself so much that he didn't have the confidence to talk to Jane or his boss about his desire.

Even though at this point it seems that our friends are doomed, they've actually taken the first step by gaining an understanding of themselves and how they actually want to earn money. As they shift to a more positive communication cycle, they will not only deepen the connection to who they are as individuals, but they will deepen their connection with each other—separate but together.

Chapter 15

How Relationships Affect Growing Money

Do not be stingy; wealth is no security.

—Egyptian Proverb

Growing your money always seems to be the most difficult area to reconcile because it's an abstract concept, and one you may not be accustomed to discussing. How to grow your money in a relationship is no different. It's a complex issue, one where significant conflict can arise from uncommunicated expectations and assumptions. As if that isn't enough to deal with, this is also an area where people tend to feel a lot of pressure from themselves and the other person.

As we've already established in previous chapters, each person in a relationship has likely grown up without direct experience or understanding of growing money. When you're in a committed relationship, you're also likely at a stage of life where knowledge of how to grow your money is just expected. You really haven't had the opportunity to understand your own thoughts, feelings, and resulting expectations to explain them to yourself, let alone understand those of your partner. This is a topic where unspoken expectations can be the most impactful on relationships, because without your own understanding, it can be an extremely difficult topic to effectively discuss.

When you have different ideas of how to grow money, conflict is inevitable. And when there's conflict around growing money, it's very easy to fall back into the Make-Spend Cycle and forgo growing all together. Sometimes this gap exists from the very beginning of the relationship, and other times it develops as the relationship changes (for example, you have children, someone changes jobs, or one person is gifted with an inheritance).

So how are our friends Joe and Jane doing with growing their money? As you can imagine, not well at this point. When it comes to the roles in the relationship, Joe has a tendency to be the "spender." Growing up in a lower-income community with a single mom who struggled financially,

Joe's disconnection to his past has led him to overcompensate for what he didn't have growing up.

Jane, on the other hand, is a "saver." Her family was more materially wealthy than Joe's, but based on her culture, money was something to be squirreled away. Her heritage has a long history of scarcity, so there was always a feeling that money was to be saved, not enjoyed. Because of this, she lived a very modest lifestyle. Joe and Jane actually apply the terms spender and saver to each other regularly, especially in anger, further locking themselves into their perceived roles with the unspoken expectations that come with those terms.

Neither Joe nor Jane was equipped in any way with the tools or language they needed to effectively grow their money. And because of their conflicting spending habits, they were caught in the Make-Spend Cycle, with Jane making fruitless attempts each month to squirrel some money away in a savings account. At the end of every month, when Jane opened the couple's bank statement, she felt increasingly frustrated about their financial situation. She would simply file the statements away to avoid another argument with Joe, but the tension was always palpable between the couple for a few days afterward.

Jane also witnessed her mom choosing not to be involved with the family's money situation. Her dad took the lead in every aspect of their finances, including paying bills, filing income taxes, managing investments, and working with his financial adviser. Jane vividly remembers the year that her dad got sick and was in the hospital for a month. Her mom was panicking because she didn't know how to pay that month's water bill. Everything around the family's financial situation was hidden, and it was just understood that no one was to speak about money.

Joe's mom, on the other hand, lived paycheck to paycheck, and while she controlled every aspect of their finances, she never had the opportunity to grow her money in any real way.

Given their individual upbringings, it felt natural that Joe would take the lead in their finances as well. At first, he accepted the position happily because he felt entitled to the job as the higher income earner. And since Jane had no financial foundation, she was relieved that Joe was "taking care of it."

The result of the uncommunicated expectations that Joe and Jane brought with them to the marriage was that one person was relinquishing power in order to avoid conflict or discomfort. Joe was then mostly or fully in charge of all incoming and outgoing money. But what Jane didn't realize was that when you relinquish your financial power, you're also relinquishing connection to your money and your partner. As time went on, Joe began to resent the role he had assumed as the sole money manager because he realized that he didn't really know how to grow the couple's money but was too uncomfortable to ask for help. He continued to make decisions out of obligation, and he was stuck in the negative communication cycle with Jane, so he didn't have a productive way to tell her that he was struggling in his role.

From the perspective of the person who is disconnected from growing or managing the money (in this case, Jane), the situation can become even more complicated when there's a change in the relationship. Let's take the example of estate planning. Many couples avoid this topic altogether. It's no doubt unpleasant for emotional reasons, but the real problem comes when the person who's holding the balance of power is unwilling to share the required information, or on the flip side, the partner is so ill equipped to deal with the family's finances that they don't even want to think about it.

I've seen situations like this play out so many times in my boardroom. The vast majority of my clients are couples. And money really is at the center of every stage of life, which means that as a financial planner I've been involved at every stage—from premarital counseling to retirement and estate planning, but also divorce mediation and the separation of assets. Whenever something happened in my clients' lives—happy, sad, and everything in between—finances were involved, and therefore, I would get a call. My approach to their finances was vastly different from one that most people were used to. I really focused on the concept of separateness within the togetherness. I didn't just view them as a couple. For me, they were two parts of a whole.

There were so many times in my boardroom where I'd be having conversations with each person individually based on their own experiences and belief systems. These were conversations I was always happy to have because it meant that both parties were in the room together and could hear each other's stories. That always provided a great start for more in-depth conversations. Even if the entire meeting was meant to focus on one person, I always recommended that they attend the meeting together. By hearing what the other person had to say, it was beneficial for both people to ultimately be on the same page.

Growing your money is a learned skill. It's not something you just figure out as you go along. If you don't have a foundation of financial knowledge, then you need to work with someone who does. But working with a financial professional doesn't mean relinquishing your power. This individual is a part of your team, not the owner of the franchise. Coming to meetings equipped with a strong sense of yourself and what you want will empower you to maintain a balanced relationship with your financial adviser.

When Joe and Jane did finally reach out for help, they found a professional who could work with them in an effective way. But really what they needed was to be willing to work together with the common goal of understanding each other's perspectives. Once this was established, Joe and Jane began shifting into the positive communication cycle—and as a result, their individual earnings both increased significantly. Together, they created a plan to grow their wealth that made them both happy.

Chapter 16

How Relationships Affect Enjoying Money

Better is small wealth gathered than large wealth scattered.

—Egyptian Proverb

Enjoying money should be fun for couples, right? Vacations together, date nights, indulging in special gifts for each other. Aren't these things part of being a happy couple? Yes … and no. If the individuals each derive true joy from the way they enjoy money, then yes, this really is where the fun can come in. However, if they each have different ways of enjoying money, without a positive way to communicate their wants to each other, then enjoying money can be another huge point of contention—because spending money is something that happens nearly every single day. And chances are, if the couple hasn't been on the same page in terms of earning or growing their money, then they're likely not going to be enjoying it in a meaningful way either. And as we already know, when things get uncomfortable, a natural reaction is avoidance.

Many couples will fib or hide the details of how they spend money as a way to avoid conflict with their partner. It may be something seemingly harmless like throwing away empty coffee cups so the other person doesn't see that you've bought another expensive drink. Even these small "fibs" can be an indication that something larger is going on.

You each came to the relationship with different influences and perceptions on how to enjoy the money you've earned. Whether they were positive influences, or not, they are part of your storyline, and confronting them becomes even more important because in the separateness, you must still have togetherness. The problem comes when no one is communicating their perspectives on enjoying money, and assumptions take hold. This brings us back to the negative communication cycle, which results in avoidance—in this case, disposing of coffee cups so you don't have to talk about the issue.

So what about our friends Joe and Jane? They struggled to come together on earning money but seemed to have made headway when it came to growing it after they reached out for help. How are Joe and Jane enjoying their money now? Is Joe hiding empty coffee cups? Is Jane's anger building with every withdrawal from their bank account?

I'm happy to report that since making the shift to a positive communication cycle, Joe and Jane have each worked on who they are as individuals and are able to effectively communicate those discoveries to each other. Jane is finally able to tell Joe about her desire to take on more work outside the home, and Joe is completely supportive of his wife's decision, because that means he is able to pursue an opportunity managing the company's charity and pro bono portfolio. The position initially meant a decrease in salary, but through the Law of Compensation, Joe's experience and passion has made him an invaluable member of the team, and his compensation has increased accordingly. Jane accepted a junior position in corporate event planning and quickly rose to a management position. She was able to tap into her unique set of skills and find an outlet for her passions. Her income has tripled since leaving her part-time position, and she knows that her potential to thrive in the industry is limitless.

Jane and Joe have also continued to work with their financial professional and are following their customized financial plan and continue to build the grow portion of their Earn-Grow-Enjoy Model in a balanced way that they're both comfortable with—satisfying both Jane's more conservative approach and Joe's interest in high-risk/high-reward investments.

Throughout this process, Joe and Jane also made the mind-set shift away from spending money toward enjoying it, which began with an awareness of themselves. They started to understand who they were as individuals at each layer of their Pyramid of Financial Influences, so they were better equipped to communicate *with* each other, not *at* each other. They started with the separate in order to come together.

As you can imagine, when they were stuck in the negative communication cycle, the way they enjoyed money was also full of conflict. As mentioned previously, Joe was in the perceived role of "spender," while Jane was the "saver." These roles were both rooted in their individual upbringings, reinforced by the communities they grew up in, and were further supported by the messaging they perceived in society. For example, Joe didn't realize that he was essentially trying to make up for the things he felt he lacked in childhood with his spending. But truly, neither of them was enjoying money at all. Spending money was just another area of conflict.

The shift toward enjoying it came when they adopted a more positive communication cycle and were able to sit down and talk about how they wanted to enjoy their money. A top priority for both was giving back to the community, so together they created a list of the charities they would support with annual financial donations—something they both agreed gave them great joy.

Jane has always loved to see new and exciting places, so she enjoys traveling. She has even discovered her love of traveling by herself, so the couple has found a balance between traveling together and Jane's solo adventures. Joe is more of a homebody, so they're also enjoying renovating their home together, including adding some luxury features that Joe always dreamed of having as a kid growing up in a one-bedroom apartment. The most exciting renovation was moving the laundry room from the basement to the top floor, right beside the bathroom, so that Jane could throw the towels in the dryer when she was done in the shower; and Joe could neatly fold and hang the warm, dry towels on the rack before he left for work.

Remember our Nixon Waterman poem at the beginning of Chapter 13 that says, in so many words, that you need to know yourself so that you can know your partner? By doing so, you will create and build the riches of your mutual, positive communication, and through that create a balanced priority of Earn-Grow-Enjoy in your own relationship.

Chapter 17

Emotions

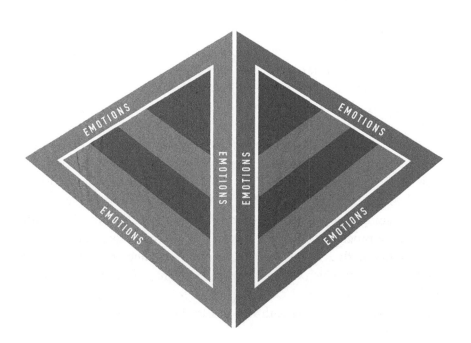

Every man acquires property,
it is a wise man who knows how to protect it.

—Egyptian Proverb

Do you ever find that it's much easier to talk about the negative than the positive? Even when an experience was overall quite positive, does your mind recall the single negative detail before anything else? Or do you just find it easier to recount negative experiences rather than positive ones? You're certainly not alone! Research backs up the idea that the negative stays with us in a different way than the positive. In his book *The Happiness Trap*, Dr. Russ Harris explains that focusing on the negative is actually part of our evolution. Our brains are designed to assess, predicate, and avoid danger, so we're constantly focusing on the negativity around us. It's not only natural to focus on negative situations; it's essentially a survival technique. That's why positive thinking is often viewed as work, because it doesn't come as naturally to us.

To add to this, all aspects around the topic of money are littered with so much negativity throughout our lives—to the extent that negative feelings, beliefs, and thoughts about money have become standard issue. All of this gives us more of an opportunity to create positive change in a truly meaningful way that is customized to each of us as individuals. Just as we were programmed to the negative, we have the internal power to reprogram ourselves to the positive. You see, everything up until this point has been external, which we've internalized without control, understanding, and awareness. Here is where we declare absolute change. Here is where we create an entirely new path forward to the most meaningful shift to the positive.

How many times have you heard someone say "Believe in yourself" or "If you believe in yourself, anything is possible"? These are common motivations intended to inspire you to make positive changes in your life.

And you can easily see how these statements could apply to the money conversation. Want to start your own business? Just believe you can do it! Want to ask for a promotion? Believe that you're worthy, and go for it! The message is that when you *believe* you can do something, a positive result will naturally follow. This advice is well meaning, but there's a step missing in this process. Do you just wake up one morning and truly *believe* that you can, in fact, change your life for the better? Maybe, but then the results will most likely be short-lived because you haven't done the work to create the foundation for a positive belief system. You will quickly fall back into patterns of negativity in the form of negative self-talk, depreciating your value, or feelings of guilt or shame when you don't get the results you desired.

When you haven't done the work to figure out where your beliefs came from in the first place, you can't be expected to make meaningful, long-lasting change. Your belief system starts with feelings. If you want to change the result, you need to change the feelings. You can't change what you believe about money, finances, success, opportunity, and, most important, yourself, if you don't know where the beliefs came from in the first place. And this is exactly what we've been working toward as we've walked up the steps of your Pyramid of Financial Influences.

At each layer of the Pyramid, we've been examining the pieces of your story that led to where you are today, but it was more than that. At each layer we're also examining the associated emotions. Think back to the timeline we discussed: Origin and Upbringing; Community, Society, and Relationships. As you walked through these layers, you recalled memories. You thought about stories you'd forgotten, remembering people who left a lasting impression on your life, and reliving the experiences that have shaped who you are today. And with each memory you had, there were feelings attached.

Remember when I was telling you how my mom told me I was a direct descendant of Cleopatra? This memory makes me smile because it brings up feelings of love toward my mom and pride about my Egyptian heritage. Or remember how I recalled growing up in a community where I felt that I didn't belong? The memories of being teased by my classmates still bring up feelings of sadness, but that isn't the main feeling my memory brings up, because this situation is no longer representative of the negative. By traveling through my own experiences with the 4R Process of *recognize, reconcile, release,* and *repeat* in mind, I'm able to decide what I associate with these memories. In those examples, I chose the positive associations of my mother's love and character building through proactive, positive choices. To create such positive associations, we first need to be explorers of our own journeys, experiences, and memories.

Now, take a moment to think about some of the stories and memories you've worked through as we discussed the Pyramid of Financial Influences in previous chapters. Where there are negative feelings, there are negative beliefs that were created. If I had internalized the messaging I'd received from my parents about my career path, then I would probably be a doctor right now—feeling lost, stuck, or unfulfilled. If I'd internalized the messaging from my community about status symbols, then I wouldn't be driving my dream car today for the positive reasons that I wanted it. Through *feelings* of obligation to my parents, I could have *believed* that the only acceptable career was to be a doctor. The problem with basing one's belief system on negative feelings is that the results will also be negative. Even though I probably would have made a lot of money in a career as a medical professional, it's not my passion. It's not who I am. And I would have certainly been stuck in the Make-Spend Cycle.

And this is the key. This pattern of negative feelings building negative beliefs leading to negative results is really just another way to describe the Make-Spend Cycle that so many of us get stuck in. Sure, I would have been *making* money as a doctor, and I certainly would have been *spending* money, but I would have lost myself because the definition of who I was came from the outside in. And it's the endless loop of negativity that breeds need. "I *need* to get out of debt." "I *need* to stop spending so much." "I *need* to make more money." "I *need* to start saving." These are statements born from negativity and feelings that there is simply never enough.

The real magic comes when you're able to shift this pattern of negativity to the path of positivity. This is what I mean when I say to "emotionalize to the positive." You can't change the past. You can't remove the messaging that you've received along the way. But you *can* look at those experiences through the lens of positivity with a perspective of empathy for where the messaging came from using the tools I've provided for you with the 4R Process. Then, when you're able to base your beliefs on positive feelings, your results become not only positive, but you'll discover your limitless potential.

This may sound easy in theory, but when you're dealing with painful memories and extremely difficult feelings, emotionalizing to the positive may seem impossible. But when you start from a place of gratitude, the process will become more manageable. The first step is exactly what we've been doing when we examined the four layers of influence. We are *recognizing* where the feelings came from. The next step is to *reconcile* those feelings by making the decision as to how they're serving you. If something is holding you back, or acting as a barrier to moving forward in your life, then the next step is to choose to *release* it. And release with gratitude for what you've learned from the experience itself. Then, perhaps the most important step is to *repeat* the positive association. This is an ongoing process that must be practiced over and over again. We are all very complex, multidimensional people, so you can't expect to change your entire belief system in one thought experiment.

It's through this process of repetition that you begin to see yourself from the inside out. You're releasing all those locked-up emotions in order "to get a better picture of who you are without those outside influences getting in the way. It's unfortunate that so many of us have been taught that money and finances are something separate from ourselves. It's this view that leads to being disconnected from money, which as we've discussed, can result in avoidance.

In very few contexts do we see the world of self-development and finances coming together. I'm here to tell you that who you are as a person and your money story are one and the same. You are inseparable from your money; and it's through the process of *recognizing*, *reconciling*, *releasing*, and *repeating* that you're not only changing how you see yourself, but you're ultimately changing how you see money. And when you're more connected with yourself and your money, this is what leads to true financial empowerment. When you start to emotionalize your experiences and influences to the positive, your belief system will start to shift toward the positive as well. And when you change your beliefs, you change your results. But it all starts with your emotions. That's exactly what we're working on here.

Let's go back to my own story for a moment. Instead of internalizing the negative feelings of obligation toward choosing a career path my parents approved of, I've emotionalized that messaging to the positive through what I associate with it. My parents loved me so much that they only wanted me to be happy and successful. Based on their own Pyramid of Financial Influences, they believed that the path to happiness was through one of the career choices I mentioned. I don't see this messaging as something that held me back from becoming who I was; instead, all I see is their love for me. The emotions that I associate with this experience are love and appreciation. Are there any more profoundly positive emotions than those? It was through these loving feelings that I built the belief that I was going to be successful, happy, and earn the kind of money I wanted by being more of myself. And my successful life path is a result of my chosen path of positivity.

As we've worked through the layers of the Pyramid, we've talked a lot about making the shift from the Make-Spend Cycle to a balanced Earn-Grow-Enjoy Model with you at the center. This emotionalizing to the positive is your key to making the shift. Basing your money story on a path of positivity will release you from the Make-Spend Cycle. If you want to earn money, grow it, and enjoy it, then you must start with how you feel—not just about money, but about yourself. The key word in that sentence is want. You're now also removing those "needs" and replacing them with "wants." And what you want must come from within you. And the only way to be connected to your wants is to be on a path of positivity with a deep understanding of who you are.

When your Earn-Grow-Enjoy Model is based on what you truly want, this is where the magic happens. Remember the class trip my classmates and I *wanted* to go on? Every element of that story was based on a want, a real desire that came from within us. And because it was rooted in a want (not a need), the money my class earned had meaning. We were able to grow it because there was value in what we were doing, and we enjoyed every second of that trip because we made it ours.

The secret to increasing your wealth and tapping into your limitless potential lies in your positive emotions. When you're connected to them in a meaningful way, you're connected to your money story. And it's through this connection that real, positive change occurs.

Chapter 18

How Emotions Affect Earning Money

Do not let worry flourish, lest you become distraught.

—Egyptian Proverb

What if I told you that your emotions are directly influencing not only how you earn money, but also how much you're earning, and your future earning potential? Most people are so disconnected to their emotions that it's difficult for them to see that they're having an effect on every aspect of their lives, especially when it comes to money and finances. It's become a cliché that business and emotions don't mix. That's pretty strong messaging most likely being reinforced at several layers of your Pyramid of Financial Influences.

But I'm here to tell you that your negative emotions are holding you back, and they're keeping you from making the shift from making money to earning money, and earning the kind of money you want. It starts with the negative emotions that create the negative belief and dictate the negative result—in this case, the result is that you're not earning in the way you desire.

Let's circle back to our friends Joe and Jane. They were so locked into what they believed about themselves as individuals and the perceived roles they were playing in the relationship that they were both being held back in their earning potential. And those beliefs started with negative emotions rooted in their own individual pyramids.

Let's use Joe as an example. He was raised in a household filled with struggle and scarcity. The emotions tied to those experiences were sadness, fear, and a feeling of being lesser than. Those are all deeply felt negative emotions, which lead to his belief that he needed to be the "provider" in his relationship. This belief led him to pursue a particular career because he had internalized the messaging from his community in school and society through higher education and media that this was the path to success. The result was that although he was making good money, he was limiting himself because this career path wasn't what he truly wanted for himself.

In our story, Joe was able to make the shift to a path of positivity, and the results followed suit. It was through his Pyramid of Financial Influences and implementing the process of *recognize, reconcile, release,* and *repeat* that the shift happened. He began to focus on the positive feelings associated with his upbringing—such as *gratitude* for being raised by a strong woman, and the *joy* he always felt when he was serving others. The key here is that by implementing the process of release, he made space for the positive feelings and associations. These feelings of gratitude and joy built a belief in him that he was able to serve the community without having to default to a lower income. His resulting confidence led him to see the value of all his experiences to create a position for his current employer where he could focus on their charity and pro bono work. This position ultimately turned into a higher-income position with a higher potential for growth than his previous position because he made himself invaluable to the company. The continued repetition of positive feelings building positive beliefs led to positive results. We saw the exact same success exemplified by Jane as she shifted her beliefs from no other source than from within herself.

Although Joe and Jane's story is fictional, their struggles are ones that I saw every day in my boardroom—individuals who were stuck. They were stuck in cycles of negativity that were holding them back in a truly profound way. They were locked in the Make-Spend Cycle because of their negative feelings, beliefs, and results, with no way to break free because they were locked in a negative communication cycle. All of this spinning was keeping them behind a barrier that was stopping them from moving forward in their lives and careers, and preventing them from earning money in the ways they wanted for themselves.

Here's the thing: if there's no meaning behind the money that you earn, you're still not going to move forward. You must give your money meaning, and that can only come from within. Again, think of Joe. The money he was making at his original position didn't have meaning. The money he was making was for the sole purpose of spending. He was making money to fulfill needs—he needed to be the provider in his marriage, and he needed to make money so they could have the life he and his wife envisioned.

When there's no meaning, you're not earning it, you're just making it, spending it, and then looking to make more of it. Through the process of switching to the path of positivity, Joe was able to apply meaning to his earnings. He felt more fulfilled in his new position and had a true attachment to the money he was earning because it meant more. He'd done the inner work to get himself to the point where he recognized his desire to serve his community, and he gained the confidence to create the professional life he wanted. The want came from within Joe. No one forced him to pursue that position. And when he got the job, the money he was earning meant so much more to him.

As you can see, all of the elements of your money story are intertwined. But at the heart of it all is emotions. You must start by recognizing your feelings, and then choosing the perspective of positivity. Your history is based on your perspective. If you perceived your experiences through a negative lens, then you're only going to see negative emotions. But when you change your perspective through the practice of gratitude and empathy, you'll emotionalize to the positive by shifting the association, starting a chain reaction. This process is directly connected to your earnings. Change your perspective … and you will change your result.

Chapter 19

How Emotions Affect Growing Money

If wealth is placed where it bears interest,
It comes back to you redoubled;
Make a storehouse for your own wealth.

—Egyptian Proverb

Now we're going to do the impossible. When you list the top five things you hate doing, there's a good chance that managing your money and dealing with financial professionals ranks pretty high on that list. But it's time for you to want to manage your money. It's time for you to want to be involved in the financial conversation. You're even going to get excited about it, because you're now able to enter into the conversation from a place of positivity. You're no longer going to feel like an outsider in your own story. The reason is because the financial conversation is based on *your* story—not just where you've been, but more important, where you're going. You see, that's where you can make a real difference. Everything else is in the past, but now it's in your power to keep it there as you move forward in the positive.

It's through this process that your earnings become more meaningful, and it's through this meaning that you start valuing money differently. There's no longer this sense of "disposable income"—the money you have over and above your expenses (mortgage or rent payments, grocery bills, expected car repair, and so on) isn't something to throw away or get rid of. When it has meaning and value, you're going to want to grow it in a meaningful way. What we've done here is shift the association with managing and growing your money to the positive. By doing so, the negative association and the feeling of *needing* to look after your finances dissipates as you make room for the desire to be involved. This started with positive meaning, because every dollar that you earn matters.

This is where I believe that you have the greatest opportunity for change in creating the ability to amplify your earnings. This want is fueled by positive emotions that build on your feelings about your earnings. You're already starting to do the impossible here by creating positive emotions through a positive association with your finances.

Up until now, the link between emotions and finances or investing was deemed to be negative. The belief that we've internalized has been that emotions in our investments can only lead to loss and are detrimental to our decision processes. This messaging that we've internalized creates underlying negative associations with our emotions and beliefs, paralyzing us and ultimately isolating ourselves from the financial conversation. This, along with lower confidence in managing our money, led to an avoidance of the topic, or a belief that the conversation belonged outside of us. If positive feelings and beliefs allow us to earn money in the way we want, then it goes without saying that positive emotions will allow us to grow our earnings in the way we want as well.

To make room for positive feelings and beliefs, you must come to a point of releasing the negatives that aren't serving you. The belief that you have to or need to manage or grow your money is one that is holding you back, causing you to relinquish your power and even causing you to be in a state of avoidance. Pair all of this with the negativity around the financial industry, and feelings of resentment develop.

With all of this negativity around managing our finances and our beliefs about the financial industry, we're consistently focused on all the things that we don't want. When that has our focus, that's all that we're going to experience—more of the negative.

Earlier on, I talked about the idea of hitting a pothole if that's what you maintain your focus on. What I'm telling you here is that those feelings don't need to remain. With a change in perspective and a change in focus to the positive, you'll find that your results reflect exactly that—the positive. This begins within you, with your financial empowerment. When you see that the financial conversation is based on what you want, then a whole new perspective takes place. You see value and benefit to managing and growing your money because you're keeping your gaze focused on what you want, and all of the elements that help to support that goal.

Understanding what you want your earnings to do for you will help you create your goals and objectives. The other meaningful change comes with what you're looking for from the financial industry and financial professionals: direction versus guidance. Now you're involved from a positive place, and you're not looking for someone to *tell* you what you want (this is *direction*). You know what you want and are looking for the *guidance* and professionalism of a specialist. The difference here cannot be understated, and it all results from the financial empowerment that has developed within you.

True financial empowerment starts from within. By shifting toward a path of positivity, you're giving yourself permission to walk into any meeting with a financial professional and hold on to your power with a mind-set of collaboration. If you feel like others are "above" you, you may very well relinquish your power to them, and this is where people can get lost in their own money stories. Through the layers of their Pyramid of Financial Influences, they've been receiving the messages that they don't belong at the boardroom table. They've internalized that messaging, and now they're in the mode of avoidance. But if you're going to grow your money in any real way, the financial industry will most likely be involved.

Finding the power within you will provide you with the confidence you need to have meaningful conversations with financial professionals. It's so much more than just the numbers; the growth has to come from within you. The numbers truly don't matter if you don't know what you want. Once you're on a path of positivity, and know that the financial industry is in service to you and your wants, then you're going to remove any emotional barriers you have and start to move forward. If you're feeling stuck in your current financial situation, the only thing that's going to move you forward is growth—growing your money in conjunction with growing into more of who you are within.

Chapter 20

How Emotions Affect
Enjoying Money

MARTHA ADAMS

Enjoy with moderation the good things of life...

—Egyptian Proverb

As we continue our conversation about positive change, we come to a point that may contain the greatest shift for you: the shift from spending your money to enjoying it—with the emphasis on the word *your*. With this word comes a feeling of personal ownership. If you've ever felt that there's something missing in your financial picture, it's because there is.

Our conversation here is structured to help you build a strong foundation starting with a positive emotional shift that will allow you to earn and grow your money by giving it meaning. The path we took to get here is important, because without meaning, there can be no value; and without the combination of meaning and value, there can be no true enjoyment. This is why Earn-Grow-Enjoy is interlinked and interdependent. Without one, we cannot have the other.

By now, you should have a deeper understanding of the differences between spending money and enjoying money. This shift in terminology indicates a shift in mind-set, from the negative associations of *spending* money to the positivity of *enjoying* money. But it's more than just a shift in mind-set. What you've done is shift what fuels that mind-set—the feelings behind it all. Even hearing the word *enjoyment* should bring up positive emotions—happiness, fulfilment, satisfaction, and joy. But as you think back to all the layers of your Pyramid of Financial Influences, take a moment to reflect on the types of messaging you received when it comes to spending versus enjoying, and how that's affecting your current financial situation.

As we discussed earlier, for most of us, our influences have pointed in the direction of spending money—in other words, toward the negative. My own heritage provided me with mixed messaging about what to do with my money. My perception was that I was being told to have a career where I'm earning good money, but in order not to attract the Evil Eye, I shouldn't let anyone know that I'm earning enough to afford certain luxuries. I was also exposed to the idea of comparison when it came to the influences of my community, and was told that I was of a lower class than those around me. Taking a moment to think about the emotions that were associated with these layers, I could have easily built my own financial foundation on negativity.

But when I look at those messages with a different perspective, I'm drawn inward to the path of positivity. The teachings of my culture didn't limit my belief system. Instead, I was enriched by the deep connections I formed with my Egyptian background through my immediate and extended family and religious community. The passions I discovered inside the walls of my school put me on the path I'm on today. My parents reflected the satisfaction involved in giving and serving others, and my surrounding community provided me with a source of inspiration that I was able to tap into when I became a member of the broader society.

These days, my belief system about how to enjoy the money I earn is rooted in a place of positivity. This shift in perspective allows me to tap into the positive emotions associated with my foundational layers. And because I chose to emotionalize these experiences to the positive, I was able to take the lessons I learned and focus not on spending my money, but truly enjoying it.

Rather than focusing on what other people had and what I didn't, I focused on what I *did* have, and from there I looked to what I *wanted* to have. Earlier, I told you about a car that I wanted when I was a young girl. To get that car, I didn't just go out and buy it as soon as I'd earned enough money. I worked through my own personal Earn-Grow-Enjoy Model first. That meant that every dollar I earned was allocated to best serve me now and later. Over time, I was ready to make my purchase with ease. What did that mean? It meant that I enjoyed that car all the more.

And as we've discussed throughout this book, it's transitioning from "needing" to "wanting" that is going to move you forward in your financial journey. Enjoyment comes from when you know what you want, and that want must come from you and you alone.

We live in a consumer-driven society that places a high priority on instant gratification. This paradigm leads directly to mindless spending and collecting things without true meaning or value. With this mind-set, you'll find yourself constantly asking, "Where did all my money go?" This type of spending comes from a place of negativity, which is traceable through your Pyramid of Financial Influences. This is why it's important to do the work and unlock the root of your spending habits. To create real change, it's necessary to get to the point of releasing a past that no longer serves and uplifts you.

Throughout this process, you've been making conscious choices. You've been focusing on the ways in which you earn, grow, and enjoy your money. When it's time to enjoy your money, you can truly do so with ease, because every dollar of this money is allocated; and from this allocated money, each decision is a conscious choice. The enjoyment is purposeful, and directed from within you.

Now, you enjoy with ease because the money is coming from a positive place. You're connected to every part of how your money gets to a place of enjoyment, and what it does is allow you to enjoy it more as it amplifies the entire process. With the process of Earn-Grow-Enjoy in place now, you no longer worry about bills coming in or looking at bank statements. You open those bills and look at the statements with gratitude, knowing that you've made positive and conscious choices along the way.

Once you've worked through the layers of your Pyramid and brought a conscious awareness to where your beliefs around enjoying money came from, then you'll be in a better place to discover what you truly want. Feelings of enjoyment can only come from the inside, so if you're not connected to who you are, then you're going to be stuck spending money based on need. Working through each layer of your Pyramid with the idea of recognizing, reconciling, releasing, and repeating at each stage will lead you to not only discover more about who you are, but you'll be able to understand what you want. And when you make decisions rooted in want, then you'll start to feel the enjoyment of money that's been lacking in your journey up till now.

Conclusion

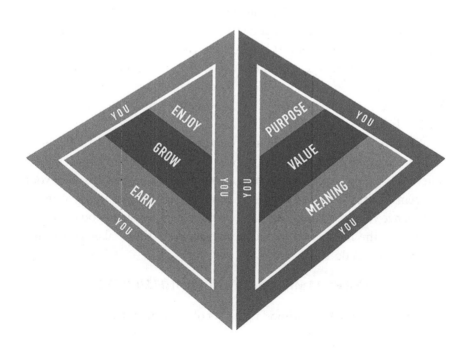

Follow your heart as long as you live...
When wealth has come, follow your heart,
Wealth does no good if one is glum!

—Egyptian Proverb

Your storyline is a journey. Together we've walked through your past, present, and future looking for a way to redefine your money story. You've chosen to read this book for a reason. Chances are, you were feeling stuck—stuck in a financial situation that wasn't moving you forward. There's also a good chance that this book wasn't the first place you turned to for financial advice. And if you've looked for other answers, my guess is that you didn't find them. Why? Because *you* didn't start with *you.* Your money story is completely unique to you, so if you turned to the outside world to change your situation, you were missing a huge piece of the puzzle. You needed to be at the center of your own story, directing your life from the inside out.

What we've been talking about throughout this book really boils down to a few basic concepts. I haven't provided you with a formula or template where you'll plug in some numbers and generate the answers to all of your problems. What I've done here is give you the tools to go inside yourself and change your perspective on how you got to where you are today. Within this idea is the real power to fuel lasting change. This makes everything that you want to do... work!

THE PYRAMID OF FINANCIAL INFLUENCES

Each of us reaches adulthood with a set of influences that we've gathered along the way. These outside influences have provided us with messaging about who we are. They've also exemplified different concepts about money. We learned about money and developed our understanding of finances from these outside influences. We can't escape them, but it's up to us as to what we do with those messages. If we let the outside world define who we are, we're placing barriers in front of our path. When we limit ourselves, we're not able to move forward in our journey. This is where those feelings of being "stuck" can come from. We continue to run into these limiting factors, and since we don't have an understanding of how they got there, we'll never be able to get past them.

These influences started before you were even born. The origins of your family and the stories that they carried with them through generations are present long before your story even began. Cultural beliefs, your ancestors' experiences, and connections to past traditions all played a significant role with respect to your views about the world. And the roots of your origins have been expressed through the values your parents imprinted on you. Their beliefs guided the decisions they made when raising you and your siblings. And your extended family played a role in reinforcing or contrasting the messages your parents passed along to you.

Your origins and upbringing are deeply rooted influences that create the foundation for your entire pyramid. How you feel about money is traceable directly to this foundation because the messaging you received (or didn't receive) created the basis for everything that came afterward. Without a firm understanding of where you came from, you could never truly understand where you were going.

And this concept is applicable to how you feel about money in the present—if you don't understand where the emotions came from, how are you going to be able to change them and move forward?

When you move through your timeline and start to evaluate yourself within the context of your community, it's easier to see how outside influences start to play a role in defining who you are as a person, as well as your relationship to finances. As we discussed earlier, many of us get stuck in an information loop, where the community (specifically, the school system) expects that we're learning how to manage money at home, but there's an expectation that the education is coming from the community. We get lost in this loop and enter into adulthood with no real basis for understanding.

Now you may struggle with feelings of guilt and embarrassment because you really don't understand the financial world and don't have the tools to engage in a productive financial conversation. But by looking at what you were taught about money in the context of your community (schools, religious or spiritual affiliations, and so on), you may change the perspective on yourself and realize that your lack of knowledge is rooted in systems outside of yourself. This change in perspective will provide you with empathy about yourself and your situation.

The third layer of your Pyramid has you moving up your timeline into early adulthood, when you're leaving the confines of your family household and the surrounding community and carving out a place for yourself in society. Now you're entering into a series of very large systems. From the media to the financial sector to the class system, messaging is everywhere. The outside influences become louder and can be harder to manage because you can't escape them. There is virtually no way to avoid these systems, especially when you're talking about money. It's here in society that the financial conversation is no longer theoretical, because you're actually participating in the system. At this point, you're applying everything you've been taught so far and making huge life decisions around your career and future potential.

The final layer that must be addressed in order to get the full picture is your relationships. As you know by now, money comes into play in every relationship you have—family, friends, colleagues, even casual acquaintances. But the focus here has been on romantic relationships because of how impactful they can be on your life and finances.

The key to evaluating your relationship is to look at the perceived roles you entered into it with. These perceptions were created throughout the other layers of your pyramid and really come into play when you need to come together in a partnership. If you don't understand where your perceptions and expectations of yourself and the other person came from, you're not only going to feel stuck in your financial journey, you're going to feel stuck in your relationship as well. As you work through the preceding layers, you're creating a foundation to switch from a negative communication cycle to a positive one. When both partners make that switch, you'll be able to move forward together.

The most important lesson you want to take away as you move through your timeline and go up through the layers is to remember why you're using a pyramid in the first place. From a distance, a pyramid can look like a simple, one-dimensional triangle. However, change your perspective and you'll realize that it's actually a very complex, multidimensional structure composed of many tiny pieces, each with multiple perspectives.

As you're working through your own Pyramid of Financial Influences, remember that changing your perspective toward the positive will be key to unlocking the treasure. The human mind tends to drift to the negative—to focus on negative experiences and associated negative emotions. You certainly can't change the past, but you can change how you view it. Perspective is a choice, and to move forward in your money story, you must choose to look at your past through the lens of positivity by focusing on the lessons you learned, and the gratitude you feel about every experience you've had.

THE 4R PROCESS: RECOGNIZE, RECONCILE, RELEASE, REPEAT

It's not enough to simply walk through these layers in the hope that when you reach the top, your life will change for the better. Recognizing *where* your emotions came from and *what* emotions you associate with certain experiences and messages is only the first step. Once you have this understanding, the next step is to reconcile the emotions and resulting beliefs by deciding whether they're serving and uplifting you, or whether they're holding you back. As mentioned, internalizing the messaging you received from outside influences can create barriers throughout your life, directly blocking the path toward the financial success you're looking for. Receiving messages from the outside and letting them define who you are is not serving you. You lose yourself in the message, and this is when you get stuck in a cycle of negativity. Reconciling your emotions is making the decision to keep only what is lifting you up… and releasing what is not.

Letting go of an emotion that's holding you back is more than just forgetting about it. The way you release it is critical to this process. It must be released with gratitude for what it taught you. Every experience and the resulting emotion has led you to the place you are today; therefore, it's a part of who you are. Approaching this process with a sense of appreciation will only serve to move you forward, because it's with gratitude that the negativity will truly be released. This process is how you emotionalize to the positive.

The most important part of the entire process is the repetition, for two specific reasons. First, repeating the new positive feeling and association is important because the negative feeling was formed over time, so the positive feeling will need time to replace what you've become accustomed to. Second, you need to repeat this process over and over again. You're a complex, multidimensional being who's always evolving and changing. New memories will continue to surface. Emotions will be triggered. Life will change. As you're navigating these situations, repeat the process you've learned here to ensure you're not creating more barriers as you continue on your journey.

EARN-GROW-ENJOY MODEL

A lot of what you've been doing as you walk up the layers of your Pyramid of Financial Influences is working to recognize your emotions, reconciling them, releasing the ones that no longer serve you, and then repeating the process. This is actually a systematic transition from a place of negativity to a place of positivity. It's through such a positive perspective that you'll be able to see yourself more clearly and make the changes you truly desire in your financial situation. A huge part of that shift must come from the language you use around what you do with your money. When you're coming at the conversation from a place of negativity, you're talking about making money, spending money, and somewhere in there, trying to save money. Each of these terms carries the weight of negativity. If you continue to hold on to them, you'll never be able to move forward toward the financial success you want.

It's under the burden of the Make-Spend Cycle where you can get lost. You make money, you spend money, and at some point maybe you try to save some money. You continue this never-ending loop with no way out. The missing piece in this cycle is *you*. Where are you in that loop? This is an example of seeing yourself as something separate from your money. You're on the outside looking in, wondering why nothing is changing. Want to change the conversation? Then change the language.

It's when you shift from Make-Spend to Earn-Grow-Enjoy with you in the center that true change happens. You are not separate from your money story. You are at the center. And when you move to the Earn-Grow-Enjoy Model, you're functioning from a place of inside out. Earning, growing, and enjoying your money is all rooted in the positive. Even the terms themselves bring up positive emotions. Earning money is associated with the positive meaning of work, fulfillment, and satisfaction. Growing money means limitless potential, empowerment, and confidence. And enjoying the money you've earned and grown brings up feelings of happiness, pleasure, and fun.

But you must carry out each of these steps in a balanced way. If you put too much emphasis on one over the others, then your model is going to fall apart. You must work to recognize, reconcile, and release your negative emotions in the context of earn, grow, and enjoy. This is exactly why we

∧
116

discussed each element of the Earn-Grow-Enjoy Model at every layer of your Pyramid. Each layer has a different effect on earning, growing, and enjoying, so they must be evaluated individually. It's through this process of creating balance that leads to doing what seemed impossible in the past: actually *wanting* to participate in a financial conversation.

Having positive emotions around your money, and having a positive result because of those emotions, is the true goal of financial empowerment, and it all starts when you emotionalize the entire process to the positive, and focus on what you must do to redefine your financial success: Earn. Grow. Enjoy.

FEELINGS-BELIEFS-RESULTS

This really brings us to the magic of the process. It's the idea of marrying the world of finances with the self-development world. When you can see yourself in your money story, it becomes obvious that changing your financial situation must come through self-awareness. If you don't understand yourself, you'll never understand what's holding you back from the financial success you desire. So it's through this connection that you realize that emotions are connected to your money. They can't be separated. How you feel about money is directly tied to your results. Change the feelings, change the beliefs, change the results.

You've now worked through your Pyramid of Financial Influences, doing the work along the way to emotionalize to the positive; and you now have a firm grasp on how to earn, grow, and enjoy your money. But what actually changed in this process? It started when you changed the feelings. All the messaging and experiences you had in your timeline created associated emotions. As you worked to emotionalize those messages and experiences to the positive (using the 4R Process), you were able to change the associated emotions.

The beliefs you carry with you about yourself and your money were built from the emotions associated with each layer of your Pyramid. For example, being told by a teacher that you were a bad student left you *feeling* inadequate, with the *belief* that you weren't able to pursue a higher education. The feeling built the belief, and the result followed suit. If you believe what you're told about yourself or your money, then your results are already dictated to you. If you want to change the result, go back and change the feeling.

And this brings us right to the secret of how you're going to change your results. You must know what you want. When was the last time you were asked that question? *What do you want?* Not need. Want. Needing something comes from a place of negativity. "I need to make more money." "I need to start saving." "I need to stop spending so much." These statements are all bred from negativity that isn't serving you in any way. You must know what you want in order to get it. And deciding what you want comes from a place of knowing who you are. Needs come from the outside—someone else (your family, your community, society, your partner) is telling you what you need. But absolutely no one can tell you what you want!

When it comes to earning money, to determine what you want, you must give it meaning. If what you earn has no meaning, you're going to lose the connection to it. And when it has meaning, it also has value; and when it has value, you're going to *want* to grow it. You're going to want to step into your own power and join the financial conversation with you at the center. When your money has meaning and value, then it's up to you to make it your own.

The only way you're going to be connected to what you want is to walk through the steps I've outlined right here. Within every step, *you* are absolutely essential. It's here and now that you are discovering the positive power of your emotions—the feeling of it all. What was once believed to be your greatest liability around money is now your greatest asset. The way you feel belongs only to you, and within it lays the secret to limitless riches.

You've accomplished a lot here! You've worked to see yourself as you truly are and connect to your limitless potential. It's through the continued application of emotionalizing to the positive that you'll be able to continue your personal development. You can now say with confidence:

Now I see,
Now I understand,
Now I can express more of myself.

Until we sit down together again, I'm wishing you all the best of Cleopatra's Riches!

Bibliography

B.I.G., The Notorious. "Mo Money Mo Problems." *Life After Death*. Comp. Christopher Wallace. 1997.

Brown, Brené. *The Call to Courage*. Directed by Sandra Restrepo. Performed by Brené Brown. University of California, Los Angeles. April 19, 2019.

Carrey, Jim. *Jim Carrey's Commencement Address at the 2014 MUM Graduation*. Performed by Jim Carrey. Maharishi University of Management, Fairfield, Iowa. May 30, 2014.

Freud, Sigmund. *Group Psychology and the Analysis of the Ego*. Vienna: Internationaler Psychoanalytischer Verlag, 1921.

Harris, Russ. *The Happiness Trap: How to Stop Struggling and Start Living: A Guide to ACT*. Boston: Trumpeter Books, 2008.

Institute for Divorce Financial Analysts. Articles. 2013. https://institutedfa.com/Leading-Causes-Divorce/ (accessed December 19, 2019).

Lichtheim, Miriam. *Late Egyptian Wisdom Literature in the International Context: A Study of Demonic Instructions*. Freiburg: Universitatsverlag Freiburg Schweiz Vandenhoeck & Ruprecht Gottingen, 1983.

Proctor, Bob. *Proctor Gallagher Institute*. n.d. https://www.proctorgallagherinstitute.com/36951/how-anyone-can-earn-a-much-higher-income (accessed December 19, 2019).

Robbins, Tony. *Unlimited Power: The New Science of Personal Achievement*. New York: Simon and Schuster, 2012.

Sinha, Gaura, Kevin Tan, and Min Zhan. "Patterns of financial attributes and behaviors of emerging adults in the United States." *Children and Youth Services Review*, 2018: 178-185.

Waterman, Nixon. *In Merry Mood: A Book of Cheerful Rhymes*. Boston: Forbes, 1903.

Acknowledgments

Cleopatra's Riches came to life with the belief of so many who supported and uplifted me with their contributions. I would like to take this opportunity to thank all of those who helped me bring the approachable money conversation in this book into your life.

I'd like to begin by thanking my husband and son for their love, support, and encouragement in this project. You are my heart, the center of my world, and my greatest blessing. A very special thank-you goes to my sister and brother-in-law for their deep care, belief, and support of this effort. Your love means more to me than I can tell you.

Elaine Kapogines of Wiltshire Media played a significant role in helping me realize the vision and purpose of this book. Her belief in the unlimited potential of those who want to change their feelings and beliefs on money was displayed in every meeting, and in the late-night hours devoted to editing and content meetings. Also, through her sheer dedication to every element of this project, Elaine showed that she is a true professional with an incredible work ethic; and I am humbled, honored, and grateful to work with such a talented and well-rounded individual. Elaine, you are truly an inspirational human being.

I'm humbled to thank Bob Proctor for his belief and support of me in bringing this dream to life. On my desk is a nameplate that was a gift from Bob and the Proctor Gallagher Institute. On it is a quote from Bob that reads: "Thoughts become things. If you can see it in your mind, you will hold it in your hand." I read and reflect on that quote every day. This book was but a thought in my mind, brought to life with the help and support of several people, and now, you hold the realization of that dream in your hand.

A sincere thank you to Bill Gladstone of Waterside Productions for his belief and support of this book and its message. I'd also like to offer my heartfelt gratitude to Jill Kramer for bringing her professionalism and talent to the copy editing.

Heartfelt thanks to Judy O'Beirn from Hasmark Services Corp for her support of, and belief in, this project. I'd like to extend a very special thank-you to a member of the Hasmark team, Anne Karklins, for her care and professionalism in helping bring the visuals of *Cleopatra's Riches* to life and for the cover design.

There can be no discussion about the cover without the incredible Tommy Collier of Denver Headshots by Tommy Collier Productions. Tommy's incredible professionalism and heartfelt care were displayed in every element of the experience. I'm incredibly humbled, honored, and grateful to have experienced the true artistry that Tommy brings to his work. That cover photo is because of Tommy. He does incredible work, and more than that, he is truly an incredible human being.

I would like to express my care and appreciation for Peggy McColl. Peggy is an incredible person to learn from and an inspiration to observe. Her work ethic, humility, and belief in human potential are gifts she so willingly shares. Peggy, thank you for your belief in me and in the message of this book. I'm truly grateful.

I'd like to sincerely thank Elizabeth Wise for her support and belief in this book. Elizabeth is the designer of the beautiful illustrations within these pages.

A heartfelt thank-you to Adrianna from Fancy Face Inc. for her beautiful makeup artistry and for helping to bring the modern Cleopatra image to life on the cover.

To thank everyone else who encouraged me and believed in me would fill an entire book, so here, I profess my heartfelt gratitude and appreciation to all of you!

ABOUT THE AUTHOR

In her experience as a Certified Financial Planning professional, **Martha Adams** has spent her career helping her clients plan and achieve their financial goals. Throughout this journey, she discovered a common theme that she was determined to change: the negativity around financial conversations. The discussion around money and finances has traditionally been met with confusion, uncertainty, and an overall disconnect. This is because it has always been a one-sided conversation focused on gathering information in the mind and creating a task list instead of beginning with a firm understanding of a person's feelings that have developed over time.

These experiences, feelings, and beliefs are in the heart, not in the mind. A person's emotional connection with money and finances is the true starting point and one that has been overlooked or even worse, dismissed. This is where Martha's educational background in both business and education shines, as she brings her heartfelt compassion, experience, and knowledge to uplift, empower, and educate those she works with.

Martha's passion for changing the conversation around money and finances has become the focus of her life's work. She believes in everyone's ability to create positive and impactful change in their lives by taking back control through their own understanding and self-development. She invests her whole heart as she tries to bring out the best in the people she works with so that they can feel empowered in their financial journey. As an author and financial educator, Martha is committed to this process, and to keeping the conversation moving forward.